High Doses of

WISDOM

Low Doses of

ADVICE

—— High Doses of ——
WISDOM

—— Low Doses of ——
ADVICE

A Collection of Essays About
Doing the Right Thing

Marian Chiesa, Ph.D.

Independent Psychology Press
STOCKTON, NEW JERSEY

First printing 2000

ISBN 0-9669146-4-3

LCCN 99-71600

ATTENTION CORPORATIONS, UNIVERSITIES, COLLEGES, AND PROFES- SIONAL ORGANIZATIONS: Quantity discounts are available on bulk purchases of this book for educational purposes. Special books or book excerpts can also be created to fit specific needs. For information, please contact Independent Psychol- ogy Press, P.O. Box 12, Stockton, NJ 08559.

Dedicated to Meira

A shining light

and Ari

A kind hearted soul

CONTENTS

✺

INTRODUCTION

Putting words on paper is an activity I've always found more grueling than gratifying. Writing *High Doses of Wisdom, Low Doses of Advice* was no exception. Despite this deterrent and squirming frequently, the book's form evolved and the writing affliction subsided.

I hope this book will impart some measure of support and reassurance to those who may themselves be struggling with the meanings of death, betrayal, marriage and assorted adversities. My intention is also to expand sensitivity toward others and provide a sufficient blueprint for considerate behavior. At minimum, I hope the reader derives some comic relief or the knowledge that "you have felt exactly like that."

I've also tried to combine the stories of tragedy with professional and personal parables, comical vignettes and injections of possible remedies. The chapters range from an assortment of elaborations on minor problems to significant events in people's lives.

Parts of this book are about critical decisions and how they relate to "doing the right thing." I have suggested that certain behaviors and choices will have beneficial consequences. This infers that certain actions be thought out consciously and that we re-examine our values.

The observations in the following pages are my own. They are drawn from professional and personal intuition that has been supported by trying to be a good listener immersed in others experiences. However, the views I've expressed are speculative and paradoxical, as they are fused with my own prejudices, observational distortions and an inherent biased view. As these ideas are filled with what seem like moral propositions it is up to the reader to ferret out what is useful for them.

The influences on my reflections and writings are varied. They include a spectrum of people and events from the mundane to the glamorous, the poor to the extremely wealthy, corporate life to factory life and the kind to the inordinately selfish. These ideas are also affected by the indelible intricacies of children, spouse (a singular one) and random events. One comes to some conclusions by some observational radar that registers these cumulative occurrences.

This book is a result of my navigation as a psychologist, faculty member of a Family Practice Residency Program, educator, wife of a corporate executive, mother, friend, and other experiential expeditions. I have extrapolated these ideas from sources in and out of my office.

Each chapter is the cumulative outcome of being an inveterate observer and having spent a considerable portion of my life listening to a diverse group of individuals. As a result of all my diverse endeavors, I can testify to the recurrent themes that penetrate peoples' lives.

Some of the chapters may seem a little acerbic in style. It is meant to inject humor into patterns of behavior that require discomfort to be corrected. The brief guidelines offered encourage the reader to apply, with reservation, the small doses of advice.

As a psychologist, I have witnessed my patients' feelings of longing, recrimination and betrayal. They have revealed to me their emotional lacerations, intense disappointments, anguish over the circumstances of their lives or inadequacies they perceive in themselves, and a variety of other predicaments that cannot be relegated to discrete diagnostic categories.

I am indebted in this endeavor in part to my patients, the source of some of my most profound learning. The intricacies of discriminate multivariate analysis, research design, and other scholarly hurdles that punctuated my 10-year pursuit of a doctoral degree did little to honestly prepare me for the realities of comforting and counseling people with AIDS, parents whose children have died, terminally ill adults or the devastating affects of childhood sexual abuse.

Some of these people have been remarkable in how they persevere in their adversities and entrusted this voyage partially to me. I have also felt a sense of being honored that people are willing to share the most traumatic parts of their lives with me, especially dying and death, and it continually touches and transforms me. This is a privileged position from which I have flourished.

Marian Chiesa, PhD
New Hope, PA
1994-1999

CHAPTER 1

Death of a Child

Grief fills up the room of my absent child,
Lies in his bed, walks up and down with me,
Puts on his pretty looks, repeats his words,
Remembers me of all his gracious parts,
Stuffs out his vacant garments with his form.
Then have I reason to be fond of grief.
Fare you well. Had you such a loss as I,
I could give better comfort than you do.

King John, Act III, scene IV,
by William Shakespeare

This chapter is written specifically for parents whose children have died, their friends and those who support them. It was selected, not to ignore or devalue the sorrow of other forms of death, but to respect the magnitude of this terrible event. Hopefully, it may add clarity to the nature of this intense grief process and encourage some readers to help others with this particular loss by showing them how they can do so. We all feel impotent in the face of such horrific pain, but the willingness to listen to people's anguish as they communicate their agony can make a difference. We all must realize that we are all vulnerable to the randomness of certain events that could occur in our lives.

When a child dies, it renders the worst agony I have witnessed in my therapeutic practice. There is little expectation that the grieving will ever be totally over. The pain, at times, is unmitigating, as if one is on the periphery of the living, abandoned in a catatonic place between life and death. There is an unceasing array of confrontations, prolonged aching or an undefined inflammatory chronic disease. Numbness is transformed into spontaneous acute anxiety. If the child was in college at the time of his or her death, every college student the bereaved parent encounters has the ability to unscab the wound. Anything and everything can precipitate memories. The death of a child catapults the family into a life of floundering for an undetermined period of time, wishing for their own death or at least partial anesthesia. It undermines any trust in life; it is a violation of the natural order that governs secure emotional bonds.

This is an unnatural catastrophe, out of the bounds of the logical safe progression of experience that we make our basic life assumptions around. The dismantling of foundations of hope, future expectations, personal fulfillment and loss of a person to love, have a profound affect on the surviving parents and family.

After this tragedy occurs, all parents become different, never fully returning to the previous person they were, which is potentially possible in other forms of grieving. The self is transformed with a revised perception of the present and a less formative view of the future. This restructuring is a long and painful process, replete with regressions and turmoil and seems so pervasive that one believes that the pain exceeds the strength that is needed to overcome it. It goes beyond the normal travails of injustices that one must negotiate in life. There are constant internal seizures that signify to the mourner that the child no longer exists in the daily world.

The challenges this presents are manifested in many areas of living. To begin with, the future changes. There are core revisions in overall self-perception. Views of oneself as a mother, grandfather or sister are overturned. Thoughts of events that will not occur for you in connection with one's child and their personal accomplishment, frequently occur. Years of companionship and the pleasure of nurturance are irredeemable losses for parents. The hopes, the fantasies and the future "investments" are halted. Children, at times, offer opportunities to be the kinds of parents we didn't have, an intimate way of re-doing the "wrongs" done to us. This is suddenly removed.

Returning to work, pursuing prior interests and goals — all of these normal activities require new formulations. Each hurdle to be overcome demands internal resources where none of this nature pre-existed or was needed before. Some parents and family members also exhibit physiologically-induced illnesses as the autonomic somatic symptoms bring on colitis, headaches and general bodily disruptions. Sleep problems frequently occur.

The reality of the nature of a child's death is that most parents keep the presence of the deceased child alive in themselves and do not relinquish their ties. Although apparently adjusted, parents in this situation find that the effect of loss on their inner lives does not subside; they show virtually no change in their preoccupation with the deceased as the years pass. At any time, tsunami panic attacks occur, accompanied by visual intrusions. Depending upon the circumstances of a child's death, mental images may occur in the parents that depict the child's anguish, pain or fear. These reminders are sideshows and instantly appear, superimposed on daily activities.

The viewing of these scenes leave piercing flashes like nightmares during the day. It feels like surgery without a morphine drip. There are unforeseeable events and places that trigger memories — a color, a common expression, the mention of a famous person that their child admired, begins an entire scene in one's personal movie of memories.

During the entire grieving process, some parents and siblings get what they need to survive the trauma and others do not. From the start, and probably forever, parents need to talk about their child — not necessarily in their idealized form, but with the difficulties that they might have had with the child. Sometimes these members of the family constellation become outcasts. The outside world can't fathom their unique pain or are dealing with their own feelings of loss. The death of a child is unfamiliar. There are no accurate texts to follow for advice on how to manage this pain, only a series of devastating dilemmas that torment.

Grief is a personal, individualistic and unique process. Written psychological theory, on stages, syndromes, some semi-orderly process, fails to articulate the trauma. There are covert expectations that, within an amorphous specified time, mourning will be complete. The social sciences have in some ways set up guidelines for this life-changing event with the illusion of normality. Yet, this form of death should be viewed as complicated as an exponential calculus problem for the lay person and idiopathic (individualistic). Recovery formulations that reduce it to stages and platitudes is offensive. Nobody fully recovers. The process of grief, particularly in this case, is related to many facets within each person. It is a lifelong struggle, oscillating to all points but at different times.

Parents may frequently experience anxiety that closely resembles inner terror with their remaining children if their child died in a preventable accident. They become consumed with preventing anything from happening that might result in another loss. Controlled by these fears, parents sometimes restrict their children from certain activities. If they can get beyond that point and allow their children freedom, they sometimes live with a wrenching tenseness for months or years. The process of fear diminution takes a long time and requires risk, internal strength and a flow of non-specific experiences that move a stricken person from chronic grieving to entering into "aliveness" again.

Parents silently believe that they have committed the most myopic felony by not protecting their child. They persecute themselves because they did not see the danger, the lack of safety, a child's depression and it resulted in death they should be blamed for. This self-directed punishment is really based on the staggering reality of powerlessness and helplessness to prevent harm.

The reality is that parents are not Zeus, nor any omnipotent God, or crystal-ball specialists. Death, even from a terminal illness, has no control panels.

What Grieving Parents Need

At times the people surrounding the grieving family have extreme difficulty in supporting them by offering beneficial condolence and comfort. Some even abandon their friendship with the grieving parents because of their own sense of loss, disorientation and pain, trying not to add another burden with their own sadness. Many people experience fear, discomfort, awkwardness about death in general, and worse than their own mortality, is a child who dies. Sometimes people are afraid that mentioning the deceased will bring about a resurgence of intense grief.

Our society is concerned with accomplishment, action, completion ("closure") and has not developed the discipline that requires the patience to allow the detours and slowness of grieving. We also have a limited tolerance for affect. Partial healing will take a long time, if ever totally and each person does it in their own individualistic style.

A value-laden message is promoted that people need to recover from their intense emotionality after a death, and return to normal functioning and effectiveness, as quickly and efficiently as possible. Yet, working through intense grief requires mental and emotional tasks that have to be confronted and systematically attended to (i.e., breaking the ties between the bereaved and the dead), a cultural norm or expectation.

As most parents would reveal, they never relinquish their profound connection to their deceased children — nor should they. The connection is permanent, and in a millisecond, with very little provocation, a memory can be evoked. Bereaved parents are continuously reactive by these inner prompts, their child's memory can be aroused by words, a place, a smell or a simple object.

The most supportive action others can take is to encourage the parents to continually talk about their child as often as they want to. It relieves the pain, and allows the expression of emotions that are always present. When family members or friends reveal their own sorrow, memories, recollection of events that they have shared with the child, it demonstrates they have not forgotten that child, and though difficult, it serves to discharge everyone's feelings. It speaks the unspeakable. In other cultures, the maintenance of ties with the deceased remains accessible to the living; the mourner can talk to the dead person, offer them treats and items the person enjoyed in life (alter to the deceased). In the Muslim tradition, which is carried out in countries like Bali and Egypt, the grief is allowed to be debilitating and accepting. The bereaved are encouraged to dwell profusely on their grief. Ceaseless mournful tirades and emotional outpourings are encouraged. Parents frequently believe that they get signals from their children in dreams, rays of light and visions. The continuity of existence occurs in events that are truly inexplicable.

An elixir of the most assuaging power for the bereaved occurs when others listen. If you are uncomfortable or are concerned that you do not have the right words, the patience of hearing the sorrow may be enough for some people. Because of a primordial fear of death, or due to their own sorrow, some find it too difficult to listen to the pain and anguish of another. But there are other ways to help. Thoughtfulness comes in many forms, and others can help in innumerable ways; shopping, laundry, organizing, putting pictures in albums are some of the possibilities.

After the initial shock, mournful parents appreciate sensitive gestures from those around them such as beginning some rituals like lighting memorial candles, in memory, planting flowers or trees, accompanying them to meetings, or taking them to lunch or breakfast once a week. Participating in yearly commemorative services, or initiating a drive to a beach, a lake, woods, or gardens; anything in nature can be a comfort. Writing or locating a poem that would be meaningful to the parents or siblings. Being there, in a consistent, dependable, comforting way, is how to be a true friend for the long-distance climb required after the death of a child.

One of the sad things I have observed is that our society expects males to grieve differently; they are given less opportunity to cry and talk about their anguish. For males intense verbal expression, especially crying, is inhibited. Men, however, of necessity find activities that help them transform their powerful emotions into a physically expressive language. The tearing down of, and rebuilding, of project after project, may remedy their suffering and discharge the pain which they have begun to dismantle through their physical activities. Rigorous physical activity also has a cumulative assuaging effect. I've often thought that if we could gather all of the grieving fathers in New York City to express their grief in this way, all the potholes in the entire city would be repaired in a day.

In trying to convey the desire to soothe the mourner's pain, people sometimes do say the wrong thing. The motivation is benevolent, but mistakes still occur. Although there is the intention of compassion, the results of a bad choice of words may actually provoke anger. There is a taxonomy of preferred and non-preferred responses. The abbreviated list below should be in the "delete appendix" of grief statements. And in any case, avoid platitudes!

1. *Be thankful you have other children.*

Each child has a unique, complex relationship with a parent. No additional child can compensate for this loss. Each child is irreplaceable.

2. *I know he/she is with God.*

It is presumptuous to assume that your faith has the same strength as the bereaved parents'. They may not be so sure of this idea, and find it of little value anyway when all they want is to have their child back with them.

3. *Time will heal this; you can use this positively in your life.*

It is a cliché, an unknown, and you're not a tarot reader who can see into the future to what they will experience later in life or how they will get over the pain and how long it might take.

4. *I know exactly how you feel.*

One would have to have lost a child, under very similar circumstances, at the same age, and with a similar relationship and a near identical psyche.

5. *Do not think too much about it. Dwelling on it makes you feel worse.*

Obliterating these intense thoughts and feelings is obstructive and inadvisable. In fact, it is imperative to go through the entire range of emotional and cognitive processes, as a requisite for the alleviation of persistent agony.

6. *Maybe this was meant to be. It's God's will. Your child has done his work on earth. He/she gave enough for a lifetime.*

Sounds like California rhetoric. Filter out simplistic and shallow advice.

7. *It has been years. Isn't it time you got on with your life?*

   Never judge the duration; it may take years or even a lifetime. This is a cruel thing to say.

8. *Sometimes tragedies can help you grow.*

   If you do not know what to say, do not fill the void with platitudes.

9. *You are both really strong and I'm sure you can handle this.*

   This is not about weightlifting. Burying your child, you temporarily lose limbs.

   There are words that can help assuage the pain parents of a dead child feel and comfort them.

These are:

1. I can't imagine the pain you feel.
2. Perhaps there are no explanations.
3. I (we) will do our best to be with you or help you.
4. This is what I'd like to do — is that okay?
5. We think about (him/her) often. Relate stories/events.
6. It is totally unacceptable to me.
7. And finally, but most important over the long term *Listen.*

Listen with compassion and patience, hour after hour, and year after year as they continue to talk about their child. The grieving process is a lonely, difficult and challenging endeavor. There are continual cycles of pain, numbness, feelings of nothingness and brief respites between the earthquakes, torrential tides and the calm. Professional help or the aid of anyone else who fills that role can provide beneficial support by encouraging a parent or sibling or other family member to grieve in the presence of a patient, kind, non-evaluative compassionate "other."

There are a myriad of hurdles, difficulties and confrontations that consistently invade the mourner's life. An objective ear, a professional in the field of death, offers the freedom of talking about your child without the concern of the discomfort of others. There is something healing about reviewing your child's life with someone who has not known him or her, the opportunity to talk about the child's problems, special assets, the cherishing part, pictures, letters, etc. Even the remembered conflicts, frustrations and difficulties are important. Specific events like holidays, anniversaries of the death, birthdays, family traditions may need more consideration, adjustments and discussion.

I do not consider this form of therapy in the realm of traditional psychological intervention, nor in any way does it adhere to the medical model of illness. It is more a philosophical, existential relationship, a being with another to give that person courage and participate in his or her current condition of despair. Comfort, openness, listening with interest and/or sorrow, permits the bereaved a place where the full expression of their anguish can occur.

There is always a search for some meaning or understanding about a child's death. Many parents struggle with anger and internal or external blame, and need to focus on some avenue for direction. Forgiveness, if necessary or possible; acceptance, at least of the reality. Perhaps the end place or evolutionary outcome is to restore some faith in life and find some spiritual safe place within oneself. Many parents, after undergoing this complex agony, can enjoy parts of and glimpses of at least a tolerable future. Hopefully, they use their wisdom to gain a view of life that helps them determine "what is important."

Children respond to the death of a sibling in different ways according to age, the way in which the death occurred, their own personality style and cognitive development. The younger child, around ages three to six, may resort to behavior changes and have anxiety reactions when separated from their parents or other significant adults. Other children might develop fears related to the inability to distinguish between life and death. Often they do not understand the permanency of death.

Older children, ages eight and above, may harbor the belief that they contributed to or are at fault for the death of their brother or sister. When children articulate or wish that their sibling was dead and the event happens, the idea that they caused the death can be overwhelmingly disturbing. Some children also believe that they have been punished by past inadvertently bad behavior. Guilt about prior fights, jealousies, or mean actions is a common feeling among all surviving children.

The older the child, the more sensitive he or she is to the emotional vulnerability of their parents. Yet, it is critical that someone attend to their loss, which is confusing and continually upsetting. For some, their questions and unpredictable emotions seem more than parents can handle.

Adolescence in itself is a challenging period of life. Certainly, the death of a brother or sister tests the resiliency of surviving children in order to resolve this loss. Parents at this time are having their own difficulties and are not themselves able to comfort the remaining children. Many adolescents, whose sister or brother dies, experience acute loneliness while their parents are struggling with their own internal lesions. Too early in life they must learn of life's unfairness and the continuous susceptibility to tragedy. Not only is their present life drastically modified, but their future is also altered. Experiences of sharing, marriage, children, the safety of having a sibling — even the ability to resolve conflicts — are irreparably removed. Family members have a hard time celebrating the surviving child's accomplishments or events. The vibrations of a child's death reduce the joy of any event.

If the death was close to a graduation or wedding, the celebration is different from the way it should have been. All the players are not there. Repression is used to avoid an inevitable emotional breakdown during these special moments.

Including a surviving child or children in making decisions regarding cremation or burial, placement of the ashes, who should participate in that ceremony is vitally important as it recognizes and acknowledges their grief. Exercising the right of refusal is equally beneficial. Friends and family, although well meaning, should eschew statements like: "Be strong for your parents. Do not do anything that will upset them, they will need you more than before." These comments decrease the children's freedom to express their own desperation. They make surviving children feel that they are less important, and further, suggests that they are responsible for their parents' recovery. If the family can manage to work together during all the never ending successions of difficulties, the severe blow slowly becomes an endurable event.

Bridge of Sighs, Venice, Italy

Each child's death is like a silent explosive glacier. It quietly moves, ready to confront and do the unfathomable, and there is no escape or antifreeze. For a time, every book, selected randomly, was written by an author/parent whose child had died. *I Dreamed of Africa* by Kuki Goldman, *An Infinite Plan* by Elizabeth Allende, *The Autobiography of Everett Koop* and many others. At a corporate dinner, I was seated next to Dominic Dunne, whose daughter was brutally murdered by her boyfriend. Socially, there have been many other people that I met whose children had died from suicide, motorcycle accidents, cancer, AIDS, and other terminal events.

The consequences of this chapter without invective preaching, should alert us to the frailties of life and review our grievances. Many of us distort the importance of events in our lives and the actions of others. Unfortunately, the potency of a tragedy or illness forces us to change our view of the relative significance of the countless acts we experience and their effects. Death is sobering, a time of reevaluation. Maybe diluting some of the preoccupations with trivialities, the whining attention to indulgences of self and the constant focus on valueless endeavors, before a thrombotic event should occur. This chapter might even inspire some unplanned act of generosity, a little humor, or instead of watching a sleazy television program, and use that wasted hour to elevate oneself, or spend time with a child or older adult.

Admittedly, there is a limit to the written word and I apologize. All I can do is feel intense compassion, listen, guide the parents and always keep their children in my heart.

Think of Us . . .

To the Editor:

> We are a part of a secret society who have lost a
>   child.
> We once thought it would never happen to us,
>   but it has.
> We look around and see the numbers of be-
>   reaved parents growing.
> And it scares us.
> We look around our neighborhood (a neighbor-
>   hood only 10 years young) and see 4 children
>   who have died already.
> We lay awake waiting for the other shoe to drop.
>   And yet we go on . . .
> We go on because we love our children who are
>   still living with us.
> We go on in memory of our children who have
>   died.
> You might think us weakened by the death of our
>   children, but . . .
> The thing that you fear more than anything else
>   has happened to us and we have survived.
> So, the next time you forget to buckle your child
>   into his seat belt, or let your child ride her bike
>   without a helmet or get into your car and drive
>   too fast or drink and drive . . .
> Think of us.
> And how you would feel if you were part of our
>   secret society.

Shelly Weller
Flemington, NJ

About grief: Books to read . . .
For Teachers and Parents

Breaking the Silence: A Guide to Help Children with Complicated Grief-Suicide, Homicide, AIDS, Violence and Abuse by Linda Goldman. 1996. Washington, DC: Taylor & Francis. A clearly written guide for adults to help children with complicated grief issues. It includes specific chapters on suicide, homicide, AIDS, violence and abuse, guidelines for educators, national resources, and an annotated bibliography.

Death in the Classroom by Kathleen Cassini and Jacqueline Rogers, 1990. Cincinnati, OH: Griefwork of Cincinnati. An informative teacher's textbook and resourceful guide that sensitively confronts ways to work with a death in the classroom.

Grief Comes to Class by Majel Gliko-Braden. 1992. Omaha, NE: Centering Corp. A practical book designed to help teachers and parents assist bereaved children.

Life and Loss: A Guide to Help Grieving Children by Linda Goldman. 1994. Washington, DC: Taylor & Francis. A resource for working with children and normal grief. It provides practical information, resources, hands-on activity, a model of a good-bye visit for children and an annotated bibliography.

Teaching Students About Death by Robert and Eileen Stevenson. 1996. Philadelphia, PA: the Charles Press. A comprehensive resource for educators and parents explaining childhood bereavement in the schools.

The Grieving Child by Helen Fitzgerald. 1992. New York, NY: Simon and Schuster. A wonderful guide for parents and other caring adults that speaks of children's grief and loss issues in a loving and practical way, with many ideas and techniques to include children in commemorating.

When Grief Visits School by Dr. John Dudley, 1995. Minneapolis, MN: Educational Media Corporation. School districts are encouraged to use this book to establish and train crisis response teams to prepare for tragedies that may occur.

For Children

About Dying by Sarah Stein. 1974. New York: Walker & Co. (ages 3-6). This book contains a simple text and photographs to help the young child understand death and to provide ways to help children participate in commemorating.

Aarvy Aardvark Finds Hope by Donna O'Toole. 1998. Burnsville, NC: Mt. Rainbow Publications (ages 5-8). A story about animals that presents pain, sadness and eventual hope after death.

Badgers Parting Gifts by S. Varley. 1984. New York, NY: Morrow and Co. (all ages). Badger was a special friend to all the animals. After his death, each friend recalls a special memory of Badger.

Bart Speaks Out: An Interactive Storybook for Young Children About Suicide by Linda Goldman. 1997 (in press). Los Angeles, California: Western Psychological Services Publisher (ages 5-10). A useful interactive storybook for young children that provides words to use for the young child to discuss the sensitive topic of suicide.

Lifetimes: The Beautiful Way to Explain Death to Children by B. Mellonie and R. Ingpen. 1983. New York, NY: Bantam Books (ages 4-10). This book explains the life cycle of plants, animals and people.

Death Is Hard To Live With by J. Bode. 1993. New York, NY: Bantam Doubleday Dell Publishing. Teenagers talk frankly about how they cope with loss.

Fire in My Heart, Ice in My Veins by Enid Traisman. 1992. Omaha, NE: Centering Corporation. A wonderful book for teenagers to explore thoughts and feelings and record grief memories.

When Someone Very Special Dies by Marge Heegaard. 1988. Minneapolis, MN: Woodland Press (ages 4-7). An excellent workbook for young children that uses artwork and journaling to allow them to understand and express their grief.

Resources

Center for Living
704 Broadway, 3rd Floor
New York, NY 10003
212-533-3550

Center for Sibling Loss
1700 W. Irving Park
Chicago, IL 60613
312-883-0268

Compassionate Friends
P.O. Box 1347
Oakbrook, IL 60521
708-990-0010

Grief Recovery Institute
8306 Wilshire Boulevard
Suite 21-A
Los Angeles, CA 90211
800-445-4808

Miscarriage, Infant Death, Stillbirth (MIDS)
% Janet Tischler
16 Crescent Drive
Parsippany, NJ 07054
201-263-6730

Resolve, Inc.
5 Water Street
Arlington, MA 02174
617-643-2424

Teen Age Grief, Inc.
P.O. Box 4935
Panorama City, CA
91412-4935
805-254-1501

CHAPTER 2

Solitude

No entertainment is so cheap as reading, nor any pleasure so lasting.
> Lady Mary Wortley Montaqu, letter (1753),
> in Octave Thanet, ed., The Best Letters
> of Lady Mary Wortley Mantaqu (1901).

The greatest gift is a passion for reading. It is cheap, it consoles, it distracts, it excites, it gives knowledge of the world and experience of a wide kind. It is a moral illumination.
> Elizabeth Hardwick, in George Plimpton,
> ed., The Writer's Chapbook (1989).

Anything we fully do is an alone journey.
> Natalie Goldberg, Writing Down
> the Bones (1986).

The capacity to tolerate aloneness in part has contributed to my general feeling of internal security and serenity for as long as I can recollect. Possessing this satisfying "interior" life has been my most valuable asset. Loneliness, boredom or dependence on others have been non-existent problems. I find that being with myself is reliably replenishing. Reading, soupmaking, doing creative projects, allowing fleeting imaginative ideas and organizing my home drawers opens my mind to many thoughts. This inner terrain enables me to self-soothe and create a private world of comfort that is a reservoir of strength in my roles as a psychologist, behavioral scientist, parent, and friend.

I imagine that you, the reader, have determined that my internal self-sufficiency is a result of early nurturing and adequate parenting. You might be saying to yourself with envy, "How can I obtain this state?" To the former observation, it is more attributable to a manageable level of adversity and a pre-existing, possibly genetic determinant. Because of family dynamics, I developed an early awareness that taking care of oneself was an inevitable role in life, the epitome of a self-reliant philosophy.

As an adaptation to my family or an inherent developmental expression, I liked being alone as a child, whether reading, playing the piano, shopping and/or even studying for an exam. At one stage of my life, specifically during adolescence, I avoided a connection to my family, yet tried to protect and mother my younger sister.

As an adolescent, I developed a "lighthouse-keeper" personality, as protection from family dramas. Yet, contradictorily, gregariousness, social comfort and intuitive interactivity were included in my psychological type. One of my beliefs is that individuals contain topographies of traits, capabilities and predispositions. Certain conditions both legitimize and prevent these facets from emerging.

Silence is palliative, a precious salvo to parenting, spousing, and professional demands, as well as a necessary antidote to life's exigencies. Solitariness is corrective, soothing and restorative. It has the ability to decrease accumulated tensions and cultivate a connection to oneself. Aloneness is necessary for growth and access to your inner world. When we are alone, we are required to use our resources to make decisions, some of which may seem trivial while others are monumental.

These monastic moments are the time for contemplation about oneself, others in your life, and reflection and evaluation. When one disconnects from the business, the noise, and the distractions, internal calmness can be generated. Paradoxically, those who are content in reclusive endeavors generally have satisfying relationships because they are not based on voids and needy expectations.

People who do not have an absorbing need of others are generally attractive in that their friendships or interactions are based on interest and not from a deficit in their lives. Dependent people are intrusive because they are demanding of others' time and resources.

Personally, as my reservoir of listening, interacting, problem-solving, sensitivity, mothering and other sundry roles reduces in content, I long for transatlantic journey, hours of train rides, and the peace of libraries and places where no one can reach me. Cloistering!

Our society has a value-laden idea that interpersonal interactions and relationships are the sine qua non of satisfaction and an indicator of mental health. However, I believe a quintessential core psychological task is to be comfortable with oneself. So many people fill their lives with superfluous activities, acquaintances, peripatetic diversions to escape loneliness and their own conflicts, in an attempt to fill up voids.

It is also a significant loss for children that our culture has been inundated with television, Nintendo, Sega Genesis, computer games of violence, a constant barrage of interactive options that seduces one to keep busy. Reading and other solitary activities have been replaced by the constant obligations of programmed events. Parents are in perpetual motion, transporting their children to an avalanche of scheduled time slots, out of some generated sense of obligation. Children must participate in a plethora of sports, dance lessons, tutoring, etc.

This phenomena, in middle and other classes, produce over-scheduled prototype A people with frenetic timetables. Meals are haphazard. Maybe I am old-fashioned or just plain selfish, but having a quiet dinner, reading a book, playing a game, or relaxing, is a time for family reclusivity and connection.

Further impediments to meaningful equanimity are the electronic acquisitions now available: car and portable phones, faxes, E-mail, the beehive of life to give us some semblance of importance. Closing our evenings is the habitual drug of television, the effortless accomplice to the mind atrophied. It requires minimum skills, avoids any creative ideas, and participation has very little relevance to functioning in a complex world. We have an abundance of gadgets that have a numbing, escapist effect on our level of thinking.

When patients or friends state that they just want to be happy, my speech generally is that happiness is an illusive riddle and I suggest they redefine that goal or expectation. The preconception that a particular event, an exchange of spouse or a particular acquisition results in happiness, unfortunately, may channel us in murky directions. It may be better to relinquish the questionable types of goals that rely on people or events outside of ourselves. Happiness is a global state of feelings inside ourselves, and is reached autonomously.

Satisfaction occurs in several different ways. For example, pursuing endeavors that require us to plan, expedite and reach a goal can result in self-satisfaction. I am not necessarily referring to mastering a project. It can be in the category of making curtains, cooking a good meal, or planning a trip. The experience may have a subjective feeling of anxiety. Satisfaction is not devoid of internal feelings of discomfort. It is enduring the challenge of the task that results in good feelings of accomplishment.

Another form of meaningful solitude is the ability to be absorbed in something that has no outcome, that is fascinating, or that allows us to expand a capacity — a challenge to our daily functioning. The state that occurs when one is so focused that all other distractions are screened out, and is one that individuals relate as being pleasurable — induces an almost hypnotic trance. The brain and its chronic dissatisfaction require that we continually learn to evolve, create and challenge. Happiness, sometimes, is based on finding satisfying interpersonal relationships. However, this is related to circumstances that change shape and is always too dependent on others.

The conditions created by our technological advancement competes with, and may even devalue, books. There is a hypotonic, orgasmic state induced with retrieval of E-Mail, World Wide Web access and games of every preprogrammed order. Residents in training at the hospital of my employment fixate on Minesweeper, a simulated depth-charge avoider. All this electronic compulsion presents a formidable acceleration to repetitious behavior and the retardation of reading enthusiasm.

Early in one's educational expedition, books can be associated with assignments, sleuthing for main themes and all forms of analysis. Grades and the potential for criticisms can infringe on the long-term benefits of reading. The question arises: Does this extinguish or suppress children's love of books? When they are young, children adore the pictures, the stories, and rhyming words. In adulthood, for many, reading is like the dinosaurs — basically extinct.

Reading is vital to acquiring knowledge, improving language, and fostering literary appreciation. Novelists do a better job than any psychobehavioral study in expressing the subtleties of family life. One gets closer to the truth of disrupted lives, competition, betrayals, revenge, and divorce in literature. We learn more when we are absorbed in a novel than from any analytic text.

Eschewing junk books written by unimaginative journalistic midgets, I prefer *The New York Times* Book Review choice of literary contributions. The characters, their dilemmas, and solutions have imprinted a source of knowledge that reconstructs the circumstances and the emotional episodes into vicissitudes of life.

Books are an elixir for claustrophobic conditions while riding on an airplane, allowing one to avoid the next-seat occupants' empty palaver, hopefully not an infant's bellowing. Novels are reliable mentors, elevating the mind in times of intellectual deprivation.

Even what is classified, in my own phylogenetic scale of quality writing is a caliber above the genre of airplane reading. Several years ago, I started a list, due to the anticipation of memory loss or retrograde amnesia, to refer these discoveries to others. In a disciplined way, a book could not be included until it fulfilled self-imposed criteria, to be read at least three-fourths of the way.

The conclusion reached, if I had not finished the book and was struggling with the content or style, it was never worth reading. As with other pleasures, I am sharing my reading list. The starred selections on the list that follows have some literary merit, in my own evaluative standards. Some deserve demerits for their measured failings and others fall in the neutral zone.

Summer '73

Diary of Anais Nin
M/F - Anthony Burgess
Teachings of Don Juan - Carlos Castenada
End of the Road - John Barth
Geronimo Rex - Barry Hannah
Mad in Pursuit - Violette Le Duc
The Serial Tale - Jerzy Kosinski
Open Marriage - Nena and George O'Neill
Be There Now - Richard Alper
The Needles Eye - Margaret Drabble
Becoming Partners - Carl Rogers

Fall '73 - Spring '74

Thank You All Very Much - Margaret Drabble
Sybil - Flora Rheta Schreiber
A Different Woman - Jane Howard
Summer Before Dark - Doris Lessing
Sheila Levine is Dead and Living in New York - Gail Parent
One Hand Clapping - Anthony Burgess
The Indigo Bunting - Valerie Sheebhan

Summer '74 (Meira's Summer)

Memoirs of an Ex-Prom Queen - Alex K. Shulman
*The Driver's Seat - Muriel Spark
Necessary Objects - Louis Gould
Widow - Lynn Caine
Of Death and Dying - Kubler Ross
Why Am I Afraid to Tell You who I Am? - John Powell S.J.
Encounter Group - Carl Rogers

Fall '74 - Winter '75

*The Ebony Tower - John Fowles
Fear of Flying - Erica Jong
How Do You Feel - John Wood
Inside Groups - Thomas Verny
The Transparent Self - Sidney Jourard
Growing Up Human - Anthony Rose
Truth and Light: brief explanations -
   M R Bawa Muhaiyaddeen
The Diary of Anais Nin
John & Mimi - John and Mimi Lobel
Alive - Piers Paul Read
The Portrait of a Marriage - Nigel Nicolson
The Wisdom of Insecurity - Alan Watts

Winter '75 - Spring '75

The Realms of Gold - Margaret Drabble

Summer '76
Loving Woman - Ruth Falk
The End of the Affair - Graham Green

1978 - 1979
Mrs. Stevens Hears the Mermaid Singing - May Sarton
Daniel Marton - John Fowles
Journal of Solitude - May Sarton
*Wilder Shores of Love - Leslie Blanch
A Spy in the House of Love - Anais Nin
Blind Date - Jerzy Kozinski
Ottoline - Sandra Jobson Darroch
A Sea Change - Louis Gould
A Reading - May Sarton
Beards Room - Anthony Burgess

Months: May, June & July (Post PhD.)
Love Etc. - Bel Kaufman
Secrets and Surprises - Ann Beatie
The Heart Keeper - Francoise Sagan
Sunlight on Cold Water - Francoise Sagan
Life Before Man - Margaret Atwood
Cybille - Joyce Carol Oates
Feelings - Willard Gaylin
The Culture of Narcissism - Christopher Laush
The Unmade Bed - Francoise Sagan
Area Code 215 - A Private Life in Bucks County -
  Walter Teller

Bonjour Tristesse - Francoise Sagan
Aimez Vous Brahms - Francoise Sagan
Bloomsbury - A House of Lions - Leon Edel
Max Perkins - Editor of Genius - Scott Berg
The Disowned Self - Nathaniel Branden
The Girl on a Swing - Richard Adams
The Unspeakable Crimes of Dr. Petiot - Thomas Maeder
The Main Shibumi - Trevanian (Rodney Whitaker)

November 1980

The Anatomy of An Illness - Norman Cousins
The Crash of '79 - Paul Erdman
Lovers and Tyrants - Francis du Plexis Grey
A Sentimental Education - Joyce Carol Oates
Cain & Abel - Jeffery Archer
Sleepless Nights - Elizabeth Hardwick
Bellefleure - Joyce Carol Oates
The Love Hunter - John Hassler

1982

Cinderella Complex - Colette Dowling
White Hotel - E.B. Thomas
The Woman Who Lived in a Prologue - Schindler
Eye of the Needle - Ken Follett
Sophie's Choice - William Styron
To Love Again, Psychiatrists search for love - Norman Garbo
Over 40 at Last - Susanna Kubelka

1983

Unknown Women - Alice Koeller
Set This House on Fire - William Styron
The Man from St. Petersburg - Ken Follett
The Little Drummer Boy - John Le Carre
August - Judith Rossner
*The Color Purple - Alice Walker
Heartburn - Nora Ephron
The Odd Woman - Gail Godwin

Summer 1984 - Nantucket

In A Summer Season - Elizabeth Taylor
Angel of Light - Joyce Carol Oates
*A Bend in the River - V.S. Naipal
Godplayer - Robin Cook

Winter 1984

*Chronicle of a Death Foretold - Gabriel Marquez

1985

Solstice - Joyce Carol Oates
*Mirror Image - Lynda Grey Sexton
One More Sunday - Jean Maitmale
Hotel du Lac - Anita Brookner
Providence - Anita Brookner
Look at Me - Anita Brookner
The Problem - Muriel Spark
Listening to Billie - Alice Adams
Smart Women - Judy Blume

1990

Nantucket Diet Murders - Virginia Rich
*One Doctors Adventure Among the Famous and Infamous
   from the Jungles of Panama to Park One Practice* - B.H. Kean
Summer Love - Ivan Turgenev
Devices and Desires - P.D. James
Burden of Proof - Scott Turow
The Butchers Theater - Jonathan Kellerman
Lucy - James Kincaid
Other Women's Children - Perri Kloss
Darkness Visible - William Styron

1991

Midair - Pat Conroy
Small Sacrifices - Ann Rule
*Silence of the Lambs - Thomas Harris
Patrimony - Philip Roth
I Dreamed of Africa - Kuki Gallman
How to Make an American Quilt -Whitney Otto
The Climb Tree - Carole McAfee
The Joy Luck Club - Amy Tan
The Kitchen God's Wife - Amy Tan
Chutzpah - Alan Dershewitz
Travels - Michael Crichton
Alone with the Devil -
   Ronald Markman, M.D. and Dominick Bosco

Ice - Ed McBain
Caroline's Daughters - Alice Adams
Rising Sun - Michael Crichton
*Damage - Josephine Hart

1992

Final Analysis - Jeffrey Mason
One-to One Experiences in Psychotherapy -
  RosemaryDinnage
To Die For - Joyce Maynard
Silent Partners - Jonathan Kellerman
Annunciation - Ellen Gilchrist
The Firm - John Grisham
*Fatherland - Robert Harris
Jurassic Park - Michael Crichton
The Second Seduction - Francis Lear
Passion of Ayn Rand - Barbara Branden
*The Secret History - Donna Tartt
Blindsight - Robin Cook
The Bridges of Madison County - James Waller
Murder of Innocence - Kaplan etc.
Moments of Grace/Lessons from Grief - Roberta Carlson
Reasonable Doubt - Philip Freedman
Memoir of a Modernists Daughter - Ellen Monroe
*The Shrine of Altamira - John L'Heureux
The Spectator Bird - Wallace Stegner
All Around the Town - Mary Higgins Clark
Intoxicated by My Illness - Anatoyle Broyard
The Autobiography of Everett Koop - Everett Koop
The Pelican Brief - John Grisham
The Client - John Grisham
Fortunate Lives - Robb Forman Dew
*The English Patient - Michael Ondaatje
All the Little Things - Wallace Stegner
For Love - Sue Miller
The Painted Peacock - Ruth Rendall

1994

Smilla's Sense of Snow - Peter Hoeg
Strange Fits of Passion - Anita Shreve
Eden Close - Anita Shreve
Degrees of Guilt - Richard North Patterson
Sex, Suicide and the Harvard Professor - Eileen McNamara
Blue River - Ethan Canin
The Body Electric - Harrison
Alone - David Small
A New Life - Reynold Price
A Simple Plan - Scott Smith
The Kommedants Mistress - Sheri Szeman
Midnight in the Garden of Good and Evil - a Savannah story
  - John Berendt
Girl Interrupted - Susanna Karpen
A River Sutra - Geta Mehta
The Chamber - John Grisham
Insomnia - Stephen King
Dr. Haggards Disease - Patrick McGrath
Come to Me - Amy Bloom
One True Thing - Anna Quindlen
My Own Country - Abraham Verghese
Alienist - Caleb Carr
Mitigating Circumstances - Nancy Taylor Rosenberg
School for the Blind - Dennis McFarland
Postcards - E. Annie Proulx

1995

Fortunate Lives - Robb Forman Dew
Souls Raised from the Dead - Doris Betts
Talk Before Sleep - Elizabeth Berg
Beach Music - Pat Conroy
Therapy - Steven Schwartz
Three Hundred Senses - Amy Tan

1996

Snow Falling on Cedars - David Guteson
Divided Lives - Elsa Walsh
Ladder of Years - Anne Tyler
The Company of Women - Marge Piercy
Silent Treatment - Michael Palmer
The Crossing - Cormac McCarthy
Objects in the Mirror are Closer than they Appear -
  Katherine Weber
Fatal Cure - Robin Cook
Lily White - Susan Isaacs
Body Farm - Patricia Cornwell

1997

Ancestral Truths - Sara Maitland
The Celestine Prophecy - James Redfield
The Deep End of the Ocean - Jacquelyn Mitchard
The Book of Ruth - Jane Hamilton
The Weight of Water - Anita Shreve
Alias Grace - Margaret Atwood
I was Amelia Earhart - Jane Mendelsohn
From Doon with Death - Ruth Rendell
She's Come Undone - Wally Lamb
Soul Mates - Thomas Moore
Into Thin Air - Jon Krakauer
Purple America - Rick Moody

The previous bookkeeping list is inaccurate as many selections were not *obediently* recorded. On the cruise of reading, the geography is blurry, the content, for some, totally eviscerated and the year unknown. A supplemental array continues without chronological order. I've deleted all the technical or popular psychology books — it would overload the storage capacity of the reader.

Resistance - Anita Shreve
The Innocent - Ian McEwan

Scar Lover - Harry Crews
*A Thousand Acres - Jane Smiley
Brotherly Love - Pete Dexter
The Infinite Plan - Isabel Allende
Julia - Isabel Allende
Men and Angels - Mary Gordon
A Taste for Death - P.D. James
The Investigation - Peter Weiss
Expensive Habits - Maureen Howard
A Woman Named Solitude - Andre Schwarz-Bart
The Want-Ad Killer - Ann Rule
Death in Camera - Michael Underwood
To Know A Woman - Amos Oz
In the Land of Dreamy Dreams - Ellen Gilchrist
Bruno's Dream - Iris Murdock
The Accidental Man - Iris Murdock
The Issa Valley - Czeslaw Milosz
Nightwood - Djuana Barnes
The Virgin Suicides - Jeffery Eugenides
Vindication - Francis Sherwood
Palace of Desire - Maquib Mahfouz
*Who will Run the Frog Hospital - Laurie Moore
West with the Night - Beryl Markham
To the Sargasso Sea - William McPherson
Memoir of a Modernists Daughter - Eleanor Munro
Anne Sexton: A Biography - Dianne Wood Middlebrook
The Sugar Mother - Elizabeth Jolly
Messages from my Father - Calvin Trillin
The Temple of my Familiar - Alice Walker
Natural Victims - Isabel Eberstadt
Anne Sexton: A Self-Portrait in Letters -
   Edited by Linda Gray Sexton and Louis Ames
The History of Luminous Motion - Scott Bradford
An Indecent Obsession - Colleen McCullough
The Thorn Birds - Colleen McCullough
In Love with Daylight - Wilfred Sheed

The Book of Evidence - John Banville
The Little Disturbances of Man - Grace Paley
At the Bottom of the River - Jamaica Kincaid
The Stone Diaries - Carol Shields
Peripheral Vision - Mary Catherine Bateson
Beloved - Toni Morrison
At Home - Gore Vidal
The Closing of the American Mind - Alan Bloom
Ghost - Eva Figes
The Russia House - John LeCarre
Recombinations - Perri Klass
Ice and Fire - Andrea Dworkin
Drinking-A Love Story - Caroline Knapp

1998

Simsola - Ruth Rendall
Something Like an Affair - Julian Symonds
Daughter of Jerusalem - Sara Maitland
Hotel Paradise - Martha Grimes
The Ghost Road - Pat Barker
Bound Feet and Western Dress - Pang-Mei-Natasha-Chang
How We Die - Sherwin Nuland
Extreme Measures - Michael Palmer
The Clinic - Jonathan Kellerman
The Woman Who Ran for President - Lois Beachy Underhill

Reading, which reduces self-consciousness, can promote growth and respect in the daily exams we are judged by. The ideas derived from books, cultivate the ability to expand our friendships. Book discussion groups have continually surfaced formally and informally. Close and passing friends can fuel a conversation by reacting or even suggesting their latest discovery.

JUST READ.

Small Doses of Advice
The Purpose of Solitude

- Achieve inner calm
- Decrease pressures
- Recharge
- Discharge
- Reflect and contemplate
- Escape control and demands
- Care for yourself
- Be creative
- Pray
- Develop healthy rituals
- Make clearer decisions
- Get organized

Finding Places and Sanctuaries

- Parks/gardens
- Libraries
- Trains instead of planes
- Hotel lobbies
- Caretake someone's house
- Places of worship
- Public spaces
- Quiet waiting rooms
- Book stores

CHAPTER 3

Friendship

Man strives for glory, honor, fame,
That all the world may know his name;
Amasses wealth by brain and hand,
Becomes a power in the land.
But when he nears the end of life
and looks back o'er the years of strife,
He finds that happiness depends
On none of these, but love of friends.

Anonymous

Traveling the terrain of life and its accrued mileage is far safer with friends. Their abilities vaccinate against the tides of transformative events, those not always predictable nor desirable. They are the curators of your past, the surveyors of the present, and the solace companions of the future. Each friend frames your landscape by implying a place of belonging as well as a primitive source that our existence has some meaning.

By the combination of listening to the daily mundane activities, and providing antidotes to fears, anxieties, those general conundrums of marriage, relationships and family, we are infused with safety. So when mammographies are somewhat questionable, children's psyches are more questionable and men are pervasively permutated questions, they administer small and large doses of support, PRN, as needed.

Good friends applaud your accomplishments and minimize your failures. By accepting the temporary aberrant behaviors and the presence of active and inactive demons, they provide compassion, an enzyme to destroy pernicious guilt. Women generally humor your fallibilities, improve rather than demean your wardrobe, and forgive the mental health lapses.

Men, all exceptions noted, frequently have their radar antennae out to scrutinize behavior that may reflect badly on them. Criticism occurs for unsuitable clothing, inappropriate behavior, too much alcohol, or some condemnation about what and to whom, you said the unimaginable act of insolence. After the event the post-interrogation occurs, legitimizing their complaints and thus inducing "that sick feeling." The sequential issues are "your dress was wrong, and why did you say that,"etc. (inferring stupidity and subtle diminishment). One knows that any explanation, defense, counteraction would easily migrate one into "Hell."

During a therapy session, I made a remark in reference to friendship that was not particularly astute or sagacious, according to my lexicon of eruditeness. The context of the statement was that different friends add variability to one's life and probably no one can accumulate everything in one friend. The patient, in awe, responded that that was a revelatory idea. Her belief system was patterned with the view that perfection in oneself and others was the expectation; one idealized person who could be everything. In reality, there are no perfect alliances, only a complex tapestry of many threads, like a Persian carpet, a garden, or the enhancement of perfume.

Gardens are composed of a variety of flowers, the perennials, the annuals, roots we create, the lushness of peonies, wildness of blue flox, the simple deep red-purple of wine cups; flowers and thus friends console the heart and propagate connected individuality. The requirements of both are care, patience, time, knowledge and appreciation.

The advantage of having a variety of cohorts is that they encourage different facets of our being. Unlike spouses or lovers, we can have several legitimately at one time (at least openly).

With some friends, there is a literary exchange, the discovery of books that merit our time and challenge the mind. With others, the aesthetic appreciation of art, objects of beauty, the impressionistic colors of a creative table setting are what hold the relationship together.

Several of my epicurean archaeologists are entrenched in culinary rigors, directly by cooking or in exploration of this inclination. These food critics take excursions to cities and exotic lands to find the most memorable meal and review restaurants. We inhale aromas of the verbal diaries of the perfect risotto, the spices in the exotic Moroccan dish, Thai, Phat Hoy Lai (clams stir-fried with roasted chile paste and fresh basil) and the magnificent St. Honore cake. Especially in Nantucket, we ravage through cook books, the food Library of Congress, just for the pleasure. It is the high caloric method of sharing sensuality easily without the worry of AIDS, STDS, rehabilitation centers, and unacceptable addictions; the affirming environment of kibitzing in the kitchen.

The attractions of some relationships are based on similar levels of complexity in their values. We gravitate toward people who have the ability to understand and discuss the major components of our life — family, work, partners in life and all other significant areas.

People see a close friend of mine as a black and white, visually opposites. We have always been able to complete each other's sentences. And she, as others, would provide emergency services.

The additional appeal of friendship is there in no inheritance of the "D"'s; the conflictual trust fund of families' legacies, either Dead, Demented, Destructive, Distant, Deceptive and Dogmatic polysyllabic Disingenuous. Free will or free choice is assumed in the choice of "comrades;" it is the expression of selves without scar tissue. A mollifying cure for family deficits resides in the freedom to select friends, and to develop a CAT scan to avoid the radioactive, the obligatory, the moaners and especially ones who do not have the same moral precepts.

In retrospect, I have had requirements or strong inclinations for the dimensions that are important to me in friendship. As I retrace and formulate those ideas, there are certain convictions from which I have not deviated. There are things I will not tolerate. The first comes under the domain of betrayal. Women who in their past have betrayed other women have the capacity to repeat this behavior, of which I also do not have immunizations. They are lacking the principles of loyalty, trust, and honesty, and have a well-organized rationalization system that does not discourage actions that are malevolent towards others. Extreme self-centeredness, like a suffocating smog, is the relentless need to require attention. They can be my patients, but not my friends; a very significant distinction.

Another group of people who I have adequately avoided are those who are stingy, lacking generosity, which is not correlated with one's position on the money or educational strata. The avoidance of nonequalitarian relationships or ones that are coercive are also categorically eschewed.

Fun, spiritedness, some strong sense of self, or intermittent levels of dysthymia (depression) are constitutional prerequisites. The composition of the high beams of friendship are with cups of good coffee, bottles of fine wine, conversation that touches and amuses, the humor of the ridiculousness of events, the company in the tenuous maintenance within the framework of living. Friends both challenge and support you.

I have not exited too many friendships because I have entered carefully. Some whom I see very infrequently are still there and some have been abandoned consciously. Although forgiveness and understanding are important, there are times when one has to sever certain relationships. The other person will not die. Perhaps they will develop friendships that may be better and ones that they can be more satisfied with. We all benefit from friendships. They are a sustaining resource.

Five Conditions of Friendship
Loyalty
- Keeping confidences CONFIDENTIAL
- Defending your friend-their uniqueness
- Supporting them with sensitivity and love
- No gossiping

Investments of Time
- Time and maintenance are a necessary requirement to sustain friendship
- Sharing problems, joys, grief, suffering and pleasures
- Taking care of them in times of need
- Events that included particular milestones: birthdays, anniversaries, promotions, divorces, births, deaths, weddings
- Regular intervals of seeing each other
- Participation in the quotidian aspects of life; the everyday and ordinary occurrences

Compliments
- Genuine praise
- Recognizing and appreciating the qualities that attract you
- Employ different methods that verify their special qualities; little gifts, notes, books, etc., and of course, E. mail
- Gratitude

Honesty
- Communicate about differences in a beneficial manner
- Avoid lying
- Give feedback that would be helpful for both you and your friend
- Address problems before they escalate. (It's difficult for me . . . I would appreciate it if, . . .)
- Use humor when discussions may be difficult

Core of Similarity
- Values
- Mutual needs although there are always odd attachments
- Lifestyles
- Concerns for daily living

The End of a Friendship

I have continually been asked for guidance on the topic of friendship and its endings. Whatever the reason, what is striking is that these individuals had been relocated to the San Andreas Fault of lost attachments. Their dominant theme was "disbelief."

The severance of a friendship is an experience that triggers reactions of acute mental pain. The chain of events surrounding the incision results in shock and then agitation. Many do not see the signals, or the signals were weak and fogged over or there were no signals at all.

In most cases, only one of the friends initiated the split. Some detached by not responding to normal requests like returning telephone calls. Aloofness and distancing were other roads to separation. Several adopted anger and a litany of grievances to justify their departure.

I do not think that one can have all the answers to life's fissures. I also believe that there are illusive qualities and unconscious aspects that occur in the collapse of a relationship. Reasoning may not be a totally satisfying strategy for comfort.

The framework that follows is compressed possibilities that may be helpful as explanations. Blaming the other person provides only temporary relief.

RELATIONS
At best, the renewal of broken relations
is a nervous matter.

Henry Brooks Adams:
The Education of Henry Adams XVI

Six Different Doses that End a Friendship
Conflict

In all relationships there are differences and disagreements. When they are not discussed, resentments accumulate. Suppression of these perceived annoyances fester and lead to termites inhabiting the foundation of the relationship. One or both people become consumed with a particular negative or disturbing aspect and never attempts to rectify the issue. It is then addressed at the moment of demolition.

In the evolution of long term friendship, mistakes are made and they become disproportionately disruptive. It may be a financial misunderstanding, a promise not fulfilled or someone's perceived detachment. Unfortunately, it is seen as a reflection of the entire gamut of the relationship and permanently divides and erases the good parts.

Reciprocity Deficits

There is a perception that one friend is more giving, more caring, more loving and thus the fulcrum of their relationship has moved to an unfair disadvantage. This imbalance in power signals to the offended member that they are being used or at least not appreciated. Extreme and continuous neediness may be overwhelming and resentment eventually follows.

Individual Characteristics

At some juncture in the friendship formula, one of the elements overpowers the balance and it goes sour. The characteristics of competitiveness, criticalness, superiority, verbosity and any other additional overdoses can excommunicate any friend. The overuse of an addictive substance and its concomitant behaviors can shift connections into the dead zone. (See chapter on alcohol.)

Lifestyle Changes

Everyone evolves and develops at different times and rates. The currents of change pull friends in a multiplication table of possibilities and the numbers do not match. Divorce, widowhood, dramatic success, mobility, remarriage, therapy (for better or for worse) can mutate and end a friendship.

Expectations

Expectations, both dormant and active, set off internal geiger counters that can result in bitterness, hurt and moral outrage. These beliefs may be reasonable, major or trivial. They infer the vagaries of entitlement. Thus, friends are obligated to respond to our particular expectations, via osmosis or other forms of communication. When this does not occur, feelings of exclusion, abandonment, outrage, corrodes the relationship. The concepts of right and wrong, selfish and unselfish, mean and kind, pervade and good will is gone.

Betrayal

As discussed in Chapter 7, betrayal is a lapse in judgement or loyalty. The actions threaten and undermine the basic trust for which there is no available antidote. Understanding or forgiveness seems impossible and the relationship prognosis is fatal.

Brief Treatments
Large Doses of Do's

- Nurture other relationships
- Refocus on own personal goals
- Seek wise counseling
- Find support
- Laugh and cry

Small Doses of Don'ts

- Blame
- Retaliate
- Turn others against
- Overdose on self-recrimination
- Despair

CHAPTER 4

Listening

*It seemed rather incongruous that in a society
of supersophisticated communication, we often
suffer from a shortage of listeners.*

Erma Bombeck, *If Life is a Bowl of Cherries,
What Am I Doing in the Pits?* (1971)

Much of what falls under the domain of listening is one or
more people engaging in a self-monologue, impostering a dialogue. This oratorical onslaught is a reservoir of words, without
meaningful response to the other person's message; the speaker's
automatic synaptic movement.

In my observation, many talkers are foremost absorbed with
espousing their adamant original view, never wavering in their
positions. The assumed purpose is to present their opinion as
fact or an unrefutable truth to obtain status of ego-enhancement.
The other person, instead of listening, is rehearsing a rebuttal, a
counter-position or distractively interrupting. These conversations are all replete with disqualifications of the other's

presentations, either directly or by innuendo. Judgments are made about the inadequacy of other's ideas.

People are inclined to debate in soliloquy, with the purpose of convincing or attempting to influence others as to the superiority of their values, ideas and prejudices. They internally embargo other views especially if they are contradictory. Sometimes it reminds one of the parallel play that three and four-year-olds engage in. Irrefutably a game of verbal solitaire. Then there is the pretext of a discussion, the empty palaver with a "code blue" cumulative effect: death by boredom.

I have been in social situations where one person performs an unsolicited speech that excludes the audience, inured to their possible disinterest, frustration and restrictions of their hostages. The speaker is either trying to persuade, verify or confirm a point in an assiduously dismantling manner. This is a major impediment to genuine dialogue.

Non-listeners come in several forms. The slow monologuer; the old rambler pedantic style pursues his agenda with the preordained view that he has the inalienable right to induce a morphia, soporific state on the singular audience. Vertigo, on the other hand, dismantles the listener by a rapid fire evangelistic fusillade of words, better known in psychological parlance as the acute loquacity syndrome. Broadcasts are loud to override disputes. At conferences, an associated avalanche occurs when a member of the audience, at the questions period, presents a lengthy, convoluted self-edification exaltation, with a paucity of intent on the acquisition of knowledge, presented by the speaker.

Individuals possess a predispositional or learned-behavioral style repertoire of being boring and have acquired a weapon that inflicts one of the highest levels of discomfort on my hierarchy of offensive behaviors. Attending an inordinate number of corporate events, and sitting next to a person who endorses the requisite canned dialogue becomes somewhat intolerable.

One might wonder what makes an individual, group or lecture of any event boring. This trait is recognizable by a conglomerate of squelching ingredients. Generally, there is a narrow domain of thought and a paucity of imaginative thinking and expression. Sometimes there is limited affect, a monochromatic emotional baseline. For others, there is a relentless self-absorption, but little connection between their real self and their social persona. Not all self-revelatory exposure is inherently interesting. It has to have relevance to the listener. I have had much difficulty with small talk like; "Did you get your Christmas shopping done?"

Listening is not just silence. There are skills and attitudinal predispositions that are essential to be effective. It requires a temporary suspension of our own thoughts and a focused concentration of the content and inner subjective state of another. One has to shift from one's own narcissistic tendencies to learn about the other's experiences, the meaning of these events, and display enthusiasm about the value of those disclosures.

It is required of the listener to be patient, delay verbal gratification and have a non-judgmental framework in order to understand another person. One needs not to confirm nor disconfirm. Listening is not about power, persuasion, dominance, submission or being right or wrong. Nor is it about taking turns, waiting for the moment to intervene with your agenda. Its essence is an attempt to be compassionate, a form of altruism in giving to another the special gift of attentiveness. It is non-interruptive, tolerates ventilation, avoids moral interpretations is curative, and is a very profound form of caring.

Another important facet of listening is that it eschews unsolicited advice-giving. Even when my input is requested, I hope my responses are tentative. I am still taken aback when several years after a meeting, someone will say, "I remember what you said" and quote me verbatim. I hope the verbal hand-outs were first- and not third-class material.

When someone offers advice without a profession of need, my skin bristles, a stewing, simmering sensation lurks in my limbs, which is caused by certain fallacious assumptions. The first, that a request for advice was ever made. People usually preface an opinion-seeking need by phrases such as "What would you do" "What do you think" "How would you handle this?" or a very concrete message like, "I need your advice." The second subtle insinuation is that one person is wiser, more experienced, more knowledgeable about your situation than you. The inference made is that you are just not smart enough, self-insightful enough or suffer from a myopic perceptual disorder. Dispensing prescriptions for living creates a disparity and generally results in the "Yes . . . but" retort.

A while ago at a corporate dinner party, after revealing some of the adjustment difficulties of my husband's recent retirement, a gentleman proceeded to advise me on how I should be treating my spouse. This individual had recently been in the process of divorcing his second wife and was with his new girlfriend. He also had two young sons with his second wife, and children with his first. My brief closing statement was that I had been married for 30 years to the same person and my knowledge, just in concrete numbers, corroborated the assumption that maybe I had figured some things out about marriage, at least my own. Seldom do I solicit advice from others, but when I do, it's from one whose judgment and behavior exemplifies their competence.

In my presumable maturity, I avoid discrediting another person's point of view, which could make them my intellectual opponent, turning the discussions into a courtroom drama of assertions and counterassertions. I prefer a flexible, less defined view of things. I've learned a lot about people's lives by attending, listening, observing, reflecting, questioning, more than espousing any rigid ideology. In therapy, which sometimes simulates personal relationships, when you accurately describe what another person is experiencing, with the combination of perceptions that helps you determine these feelings, they generally respond in amazement, excitement, relief and say, "That's exactly right!" It mystifies people that they can be simply understood.

In order to listen effectively, one must be attuned to what is *not* said — the pauses, the intervals between words, the speaker's facial movements are all clues — and to resist quick verbal interruptions. There are many hidden layers beneath peoples' words and the sensitive listener ferrets out the true meanings.

We need to attend better to the meaning of our conversations. Mature listeners, not necessarily an age-related ability, offer less dogmatic, less inflamed, and fewer opposing opinions. Everyone can cultivate and improve their abilities in listening to others. It is fundamental to our connections to others, and developing this capacity ends in wisdom that can make relationships fuller and more satisfying, at best.

Listening
Causes and Cures of the Acute Failure of Listening

Listening failure is due to:

1. People don't think listening is a vital ability
2. The belief that it comes naturally
3. The interference of emotions such as anxiety and anger
4. Lonely individuals or those who lack adequate interpersonal interaction compensate by talking
5. Family members did not model or understand the value of this skill
6. External influences like the media demonstrate bombastic styles that constantly interrupt
7. High attention requirements preclude listening

8. Certain particular conversational styles are not conducive to becoming a good listener

Small doses of advice for those considering ----- Listening

P's & Q's of Listening:

Purpose (listening matters, it is the Heart of the Matter)

1. Learn more about others
2. Form of potent caring
3. Advances relationships, business, professional and personal
4. Consoles others
5. Demonstrates maturity
6. Promotes respect for you
7. Manages conflict

Premeditated Listening

1. Preplan (I will try to listen more to ----)
2. Consciously organize ------
3. Increase the amount and quality of listening

Pay Attention

1. Looking directly is a precondition to listening
2. Intersperse small words
3. Perceive the emotional undercurrents
4. Remove all obstacles — cellular phones, beepers
5. Limit the distractions (looking at others)
6. Monitor your emotional responses

Quit
- Talking
- Interrupting
- Being rigid
- Changing the subject
- Giving advice
- Advancing your opinion
- Being reactive
- Scanning the environment
- Feigning understanding
- Taking an adversarial position
- Being right
- Rejecting
- Being defensive
- Winning
- Analyzing

Practice
- Silence
- Interest in others
- Comments like: That's terrible, wonderful, strange
- Ways for a person to continue talking
- Patience
- Acknowledging the other person's view
- Attention, appreciation and affirmation

Questions
1. Ask questions that follow the person you are listening to — Then what happened?
2. Clarify briefly how the other person might perceive the situation or the feeling

3. Agree with some parts and then question

4. Ask yourself questions (What would that be like?) (What are they trying to tell me?)

5. Admit you don't understand and continue requesting more information

CHAPTER 5

Generosity

*We ourselves feel that what we are doing is just
a drop in the ocean. But if that drop was not
in the ocean, I think the ocean would be less
because of that missing drop. I do not agree
with the big way of doing things.*
> Mother Teresa (b.1910), Albanian-born Roman
> Catholic missionary: *A Gift for God* (1975).

*GIVING: Real giving had its joy in imagining
the joy of the receiver. It means choosing,
expending time, going out of one's way,
thinking of the other as a subject: the opposite
of distraction.*
> Theodore W. Adorno (1903-1969), German
> philosopher, sociologist and music critic:
> *Minima Moralia* (1951; tr. 1978), Ch. 21.

*The fragrance always remains in the hands
that give the rose.*
> Heda Bejar, *Peacemaking Day by Day* (1989).

Generosity has been minimally discussed in psychological literature and is generally subsumed under religious tenets and dogmas. As the behavioral sciences are weighted on diagnosing disorders, in both training and treatment, the development and expression of altruistic tendencies is a syndrome of remission. Professionals in the fields of psychiatry and psychology, look for deficits and their remedies. Parallel emphasis occurs in the media as the public is deluged with stories about governmental and personal dishonesty and mesmerizing murder cases and their outcomes. Altruism rarely makes headlines.

The intrigue about individuals who exhibit the quality of generosity and those who are generally devoid of it has been an evolving interest. As this trait has been researched as part of a broad spectrum of developmental behavior, my observations are speculative about the development of characteristics that allow certain people to give of themselves — gifts, time, food, assistance, and in other forms — in an uncalculating, thoughtful way.

The endeavor to understand the factors that encourage the potential for altruism has led to some unclear, and at times, contradictory formulations regarding the antecedents of generosity. The following is a condensed theory of how generosity develops and a personal definition of the behaviors that may be included in this summary.

This chapter reflects my bias; my own moral consensus. I admit that my tolerance is low for individuals deficient in this characteristic. Knowing my prejudice, take these opinions from the blend of brief ruminations and explore the dimensions of them in the context of your own philosophy of life.

Fundamental to any acquired behavior, is the experience in the family. Modeling, a form of learning, is a socialization process by which children develop certain patterns of acting. When family members, parents, grandparents or other powerful adults model and consciously encourage generosity, it is then internalized as a valuable component to interpersonal satisfaction. By modeling or indirect teaching, commenting on the behavior, encouraging it in a consistent way and observing one's parents, generosity (although not an inheritable trait) provides an internal sense of goodness, as nontangible rewards occur.

Parents who value this quality are themselves generous and verbally support those acts. Their children develop a sensitivity and concern for others and affiliative needs become more important than their individualistic competitive ones. It is a quality that may develop into part of their core personality structure.

When acts of kindness occur in families and children can observe their benefit, an outcome may be emotional satisfaction by displaying this behavior. In some ways, it is a subtle persuasion to foster a child's capacity to be unselfish. Among the possible causal results are the development of a good character that values affiliation with others. There may also be overt disapproval of selfishness. A child will quickly respond to the approval of being generous if when sharing, or relinquishing something (age appropriate), praise occurs.

If competition is stressed — winning at any cost — being better than others, or outdoing your peers, it is logical that generosity is undervalued and discouraged. One does not get accolades for giving and sharing, especially in school. Getting better grades as evidenced on a report card, being more popular, and excelling at sports, often take precedence over other valuable traits. Altruism is often hidden within areas that are given less value, like citizenship. One would think that there would be incentive to teach and act with empathy; It is a powerful social bond.

Although it may appear paradoxical, when children grow up in a restrictive, ungiving environment, they may consciously develop the attribute that was missing because of experiencing an emotional deficit. Many times I have heard parents, patients and friends say that because something was devalued in their childhood, they have tried to incorporate that into their own child-rearing practices. There is also the possibility that a distant relative or neighbor displayed that quality, which may have influenced the child's future behavior.

Although some parents or families give very little, their children are very giving. Other parents frequently indulge, yet their children are selfish, uncaring and give the least of themselves. Also in adolescence, when there is a determination not to be like parents, and to reject or do things differently, altruistic behavior may develop in families where this behavior has not been taught or valued.

The true instinct for generosity is not an act designed to receive praise, recognition nor for self-aggrandizement. It is not correlated with the amount of money one has, lifestyle, education or religious orientation. Generosity cannot be calculated at pre-ordained events where one is obligated to adhere to some social expectation of gift giving. There are sufficient criteria, with some fluctuations for weddings, birthdays, Bar Mitzvahs and holidays. It requires no balance sheet, no IRS ledger, no act of programmed deliberation or superiority. Buying a round of drinks for strangers at a bar, a bravado deposit under the influence, is ersatz giving. Monetary incentives for friendship and/or power signals lagging motivation. What it also eschews is the approval quotient. This is the implied or even verbalized, "Look what I've given you; gratefulness and appreciation should be forthcoming." That is what I label as the premeditated potential when one ultimately expects praise or approval. Investments with a long- or short-term dividend or simple pay-off are not identifiable characteristics.

It is not quid pro quo, which means it is not an equation that has to be equally balanced or a reservoir of reciprocal obligation. The freedom underlying generosity is that if you have given a gift or done something for another person, you should not expect future payment. When a gift is given with some subtle coercion, the act is dissolved and/or diluted. It is the stereotypical guilt we accuse mothers of when it seems they are saying, "Look what I have done for you." Or, "Be grateful," "Call me every day," etc.

However, I must add a minor caveat to the prior and later description; with a person who is chronically giving, despite some situations where they are taken advantage of, certain limits should be imposed. Several individuals are takers and that inequality only prevents them from changing and recognizing a fundamentally flawed disposition.

Generosity and self-interest are not mutually exclusive. They co-exist in people's relationships with their families, friends and the outside world. A person judged to be generous is not a martyr and regulates a healthy balance between giving and taking. Their acts of generosity are not self-sacrificing nor extraordinary, and should have boundaries.

Essentially, generosity is connected to benevolence, or the ability to express genuine altruism and love. These acts generate joy, excitement in giving people pleasure, and become metaphors for care. Sometimes the acts are spontaneous; at other times they require thoughtfulness.

People considered generous are natural, astute observers and take mental notes as to the predilections of others. The recipient knows that there are no obligations, hidden agendas, no ultimate eulogizing, or any variant of accruing interest rates.

It is a behavior that sometimes does more than expected, combined with a caring and spontaneous quality. It takes acute observational skills and an interpersonal radar. It is the instinct for knowing "the right thing to do at the right time." There are certain manifestations of this quality — making a special card, preparing a meal, creating a gift — helping someone move, anything that requires time or skill. The thoughtfulness occurs because you have listened and understood some things about another person. Equally important is the ability to comprehend the world from another person's perspective offering a credit of kindness.

Although not directly opposite of generosity, selfishness, cheapness, frugality are words to describe traits that likewise have certain definitions and effects on others. There are clear-cut instances and striking behavior of individuals whose reflexive responses are in the wrong direction.

People who are devoid of generosity are self-absorbed, narcissistic and rigid in their patterns of interrelating to others. They are people who pay less when the dinner bill arrives because their entree was less and spend the latter part of the evening itemizing each person's individual contribution. In everyone's life there are people that fit the descriptions, but display it in other ways. Their lives are selfish and unbalanced on the taking side of the equation. We show our distaste culturally for this behavior in our language as people with these qualities are characterized with words such as "cheap," "tightwad," "moocher," "selfish," "the takers," and "misers."

Although greediness or selfishness arouse negative feelings in others, these reactions do not seem to act as a deterrent. These personality characteristics are deemed as peculiar. Some individuals just are descriptively selfish, ungiving, and their lives are on the taking side of all equations. In fact, people who have little understanding of themselves display a sense of entitlement, a kind of "deservedness" that communicates an "expectedness" from others. We notice odd bits of behavior which are clues to hazardous mistakes that individuals make regarding money. They are hypoxix decisions, without the air or rightness or even simple manners.

The visceral and verbal responses on the part of others range from abhorrence to laughing at the behavior, indicating a lack of respect for the person exhibiting it. The effect on others may be an automatic response of aversion. It then is a challenge to overcome the negative thoughts and feelings by trying to understand

why the person has acted with such blatant self-interest. Cheapness is dismantling. One has to resolve problems created by it. The reverberating effects can sour an event or negate a gift.

It is harder to like people who are ungiving. It is difficult to attach to a person who has a propensity for selfishness. When others are not at least minimally sensitive, it is disappointing and thus withdrawal tactics occur. In every group — family, friends, business associates, religious affiliations — one can easily identify the people who have those characteristics.

I do not want to create a false dichotomy and distort the concepts. There are the people who are selectively frugal. If they are with others who are financially in better positions, the expectation is that the richer should "foot the bill." There are others whose motivating force is retaliatory. They believe that you did something hurtful to them and they act out this conflict in an indirect way.

What I hope might emerge from this sentiment is the belief that altruistic behaviors are within most people's reach. This is not a fixed dimension nor a function of some biological lucky accident. Much of what I am discussing does not involve sacrifice. We can continue to make excuses and be very proficient at doing so; or we can change our ideas about ourselves, bleach out our past history by improving on our present, and learn to be more discerning about the spectrum of choices we have. The next few ideas do not aim to tell you what and how to do things; it is only a blueprint outline to alert readers to what they might consider.

- The gift you bring belongs to the recipient. If they choose to recycle it by giving it to someone who would appreciate it or needs it more, do not be disturbed by this.
- When giving a gift of money, it should be reasonable, respectful, appropriate and within your financial means as people generally understand financial constraints.
- Do not continuously ask how the recipient likes the gift.

- Pay attention to the likes and dislikes of the person you are giving the gift.
- If you contribute food, wine or other edible items to an event, do not ask for what is not consumed. Never leave with what is left over unless the host insists you take them — and does so in a sincere, convincing manner.
- If one tries to do something good and the unintentional consequences result in a bad outcome, it is the initial deed that is important.
- When in doubt, give a gift certificate to a nice department, good or book store. It is a considerate way to say Thank You.
- Gifts are not about perfection.
- Generosity and its opposite manifestations are evidenced in non-monetary categories. The giving of time, and concern for others is a generous act.
- Teach your children, relatives, co-workers to be concerned about others.
- Listening is an act of generosity.
- Finally, we are judged by the totality of our traits. If you cannot find a way to be generous, balance this limitation with other dimensions. Loyalty and honesty may weight the effect you have on others.

CHAPTER 6

Alcohol

*Alcohol is a good preservative for everything
    but brains.*
    Mary Pettibone Poole, A Glass Eye at a Keyhole
    (1938)

*Alcoholism isn't a spectator sport. Eventually
    the whole family gets to play.*
    Joyce Rebeta-Burditt, The Cracker Factory
    (1977)

*Maybe it picks you up a little bit, but it sure
    lets you down in a hurry.*
    Betty Ford, with Chris Chase, The Time of My
    Life (1978)

On the subject of drinking and addiction, I have conducted
conferences for physicians on the recognition and treatment of
alcoholism in the primary care setting. Physicians realize that
many people do not adhere to medical regimens and are initially unsuccessful in their attempts to limit alcohol consumption.
The concern I have, hopefully transmitted, is that physicians

should be more sensitive to the reasons that individuals continue their unhealthy behavior.

Many experts in the field are recovering alcoholics and address the problem differently. Instead of reiterating the purview of the chemical assistance authorities, I decided to write about some scenes occurring two feet from where I have been idly and illegally observing. These are not exaggerated stories about the wild elation orbiting around alcohol. The examples are to alert the reader to the seduction of liquor, whatever form or disguise it takes. Hopefully, this portrayal and chapter is received with understanding and not perceived as criticism.

For some, compulsive drinking is a prison with revolving doors — no guards, but a lifelong sentence, a recycling infectious disease. The book stores and libraries are filled with stories about intoxication with personal confessions, and the story of the ultimate reformation, Alcoholics Anonymous, AA — or other forms of help. The most recent best seller by Carolyn Knapp, *Drinking, a Love Story*, chronicles her 20 year love affair with alcohol. It is a startling honest memoir that reveals the secret family myths and destructive relationships that go hand in hand with drinking.

Alcohol is the siren seducer, calling regularly, tightening the grip, and burying you before you knew you were dead. It sings a sweet lullaby while ravishing your life. As ridiculous as the question may be: Why do people idolize this unmerciful fermented liquid?

People drink because of the belief that alcohol enhances certain experiences: social interactions, sexual experiences and general likableness. These assumptions are based on the widespread perception that with alcohol, shyness decreases; we are more entertaining, lucid, and generally less inhibited than we are in our "non-assisted" state. Alcohol is believed to modulate people's negative view of themselves and their feelings of inadequacy.

This powerful perception is supported by the association of alcohol with pleasure, relief, fun, abandonment and celebratory endeavors. In all sectors of life, the message is that we not only need this self-soothing drink, but we deserve it, as a reward for working and living in a stressful society. It provides comfort.

The rich, famous, powerful and aspiring hopefuls celebrate with the most expensive champagnes, the best vintage scotch, and all the accouterments of Baccarat-filled liquor. Men seduce women with Dom Perignon and vice versa.

In reality, alcohol intoxication has been an excuse for reprehensible behavior that involves aggression, abuse, accidents and embarrassment for family members and friends. The behavior witnessed is humiliating for both the drinker and the observers.

Medical consequences range from nonspecific symptoms such as fatigue and abdominal pain to more dramatic manifestations: chronic liver disease, gastritis, acute pancreatitis, and other medical complications. Warnings should say "The next drink: cancer of the mouth, oropharynx and esophagus."

Our society endorses the pursuit of happiness, eradication of pain, and remedies for any uncomfortable feelings. There is also the belief that something outside ourselves will abate the sources of our disquiet. Money, food, endless acquisitions, and new jobs will result in internal satisfaction.

As it assists with the modulation of emotional states, in certain circumstances, alcohol is a quick pain reliever. Alcohol induces euphoria, a place that escapes captivity by the demons that create the undercurrents of dissatisfaction. This depository of undefined malaise, and extortionist inadequacies are soothed by the anesthetic quality of alcohol with its temporary relief. Ennui, which diminishes the capacity to feel excitement, is quelled by the physiological changes induced by alcohol. Feelings of loneliness may be reduced or muted.

Also, there is a subtle suggestion that alcohol makes one witty, charming, less inhibited, lucid and appear more intelligent — obliterating our perceived flaws. This palliative liquid is relatively inexpensive, easily obtainable, encouraged and is associated with the rites of abandonment. An additional supposition is epitomized in the movies when it is depicted as a reward after a long day of tedious work or a successful acquisition.

However, tension-altering effects on people are extremely variable. They are related to individual gender, weight, food intake and generally mediated by personality. The logic, although paradoxical, promises mental attractiveness, relief, emotional highs, without side effects.

This reasoning, with less than cerebral exactitude, has not been generally verified. On many occasions it engulfs like a tornado, into spiraling distress that includes guilt, recriminations, aggression, and for chronic users, retards development. After consumption and resulting blackouts, and/or inappropriate behavior, the drinker is generally remorseful, shamed or has no recollection of the less than elegant actions of the prior evening. Many chronic drinkers inflict discomfort, anger, become self-centered, and engage in behavior that is inexcusable when sober. They march loudly, dramatically, with full attention to themselves. The dramatic presentations amplify the performance and compel others to respond in some way.

Alcoholism in families deprive children of a sense of safety and the benefit of having parents fully present emotionally and physically. Verbal abuse is common, emotional neglect is constant. It is a slow assassination of family life.

There are cycles of fear, avoidance of the person who is drinking, constant disappointments and blame. Everyone is waiting for the fire drill to start. There is a legacy of depression, anxiety and a veritable trust fund of long-acting problems.

Alcoholism is a heterogeneous illness with various definitions and behavioral manifestations. Thus, individuals and families can create loopholes to justify its existence, which are characterized by denial.

As with all addictions, one needs to look at the issue of control. Alcohol is the ruler; — the dominating character. You can't say "No," or "I'll postpone this for another time." The craving and desire demands you drink, continually seducing you. There is a preoccupation about where, when, availability, and other mental formulations about drinking. This powerful, yet vague state of discomfort, slowly and cunningly persists and takes one prisoner. It is a tornado, never seen on the horizon, and which twists the drinker into an abysmal hole. It is a hostage-taker causing extensive suffering — the tormented lover or the disruptive affair.

In particular, women believe that they are less inhibited sexually with the assistance of a drink or two, or at times, the consumption of an entire bottle. This disinhibitory affect results in relaxation, abandonment and an escape from a more normal, daily mental and physiological state.

Alcoholism is a complex disorder. The dependence on alcohol may be related to an underlying depression or self-treatment of anxiety. Since the literature on the disease occupies a strong hold in most libraries and book stores, reiterating well-documented information was not my intention.

Treatments range from regular attendance at AA meetings to inpatient and outpatient counseling. Spouse programs offered by Al-Anon, individual and family therapy are other sources of assistance. When an individual who lives with an addicted person seeks help, he or she is making a significant statement to themselves and their families. If a spouse is concerned, initially one can discuss this with a family physician; an important resource person in navigating the fog that alcohol can create.

There are many swimmers in these waters of invisible, alluring sharks, but let the drinker beware; the strong currents will eventually pull the drinker and his family into a sea of disaster.

The following are alcohol allegories, portraits of adoration of this liquid in one's life. It is meant to describe its power and seduction.

Alcohol I

At America, a restaurant in Union Station, Washington,

D.C., my usual auditory voyeuristic self unabashedly listened to three couples nostalgically reminisce about their alcoholic binges. They were united in the joys of their past quantitative consumption, each eliciting their heroic performance including the volume of liquid, the type of inebriation, and the resultant hangovers.

Sequentially, and competitively, they each commanded their friends' attention describing in grandiose detail, their diverse talents in alcohol accomplishment: Each were rewarded by laughter appropbrium — a kind of group bonding experience — the elaborate nostalgia for a binding history.

I was incredulous as the group relived the past rites of passage and climbed the ascending ladder of approval. This transformation into the regressive, rebellious youth reoccurred at the table as they continued to order drinks. My reaction was not out of moral indignation nor criticism, for I have also suffered the effects of post-alcohol consumption, but more out of compassion.

This naturalistic observation left me with a sense of sadness. Alcohol was central to the re-creation of the past abandonments, a reverie for lost youth, the brief remedy for the burden of adult responsibility or some sterility of existence and, the evasion of the arduous, repetitive tasks that the passage of time creates. Perhaps adult life is repressive. Did alcohol play such an important part in their lives that they could talk of nothing else — A's on tests, a brilliant professor? Intellectual challenge or scholarly endeavors seemed to afford far less pleasure.

Alcohol II

In a store on Nantucket, which epitomizes a typical island event, my eavesdropping on a conversation probably could be duplicated by other locals on this island. Several people were assiduously planning their evening, carefully dividing up the responsibilities of purchasing lemons, limes, olives, and specified brands or categories of alcohol; an elaborate planning board of liquor consumption. Food was not mentioned.

Where there are codes of dress and behavior that encourage sameness and where interactions are monochromatic, the use of alcohol legitimizes any emotional deviation from the norm. As there are specifications for acceptable outer life, people become masters of restrictions, a sublime repression. Drinking has a restorative power for spontaneity, as it siphons off control and releases accumulated pressures with the illusion of respectability. The anodyne of modulating chemicals creates physical sensations that mimic relaxation, forming a curative conduit from dullness to excitement. In some strata of society where there is a suppression of intense emotion, alcohol, with its disinhibitory effects, legitimizes the escape from sameness and the taboo against arousing feelings.

The climate of conformity enforced by rules and regulations of family functioning is expressed in statements like "don't raise your voice," "be polite," "do not speak until spoken to," and an accumulation of repressive behaviors. As normal tensions arise and gather momentum, storage becomes more difficult. Alcohol releases the pressure, in a socially condoned atmosphere. Drinks before, during and after dinner is a norm and highly encouraged by others.

There is the appeal of the loss of oneself, in terms of time and responsibilities; a temporary leaving of an expedition into soft obliteration. In addition, there is the Bacchaninial aura of sexual, erotic freedom. Thus, there is an occasional liberation of, and what psychologists have labeled as, "regression in service of the ego."

Unfortunately, the waters are dangerous and the quiet undertow delivers one to unexpected places. The outcomes resemble campaigns of fights, accidents, and murder with cars as the weapon. A high incidence of violence in tandem with alcohol evolves. Fatigue, dull and pained senses and regurgitation are the post-binge wake. It elaborately devours, the incubation of the condor.

Small Doses of Information
Alcoholism Warning Signs
- Blackouts
- Accidents
- Personality changes
- Increased consumption
- Altercations
- Interpersonal, family or work problems
- Withdrawal symptoms: nausea, restlessness, tremors
- Lack of control
- Driving under the influence of alcohol

Consult
- Physician
- Clergy
- Friends
- Hospital
- Mental health facility
- A.A.
- Counselor
- Psychologist
- Employee Assistance Program (EAP)
- National Council on Alcoholism

Treatments and Resources
- A.A.
- Al-Anon
- Residential facilities
- Private centers (Betty Ford)
- Local hospitals

Dealing With the Problem Drinker
- Try to remain calm
- Confide in someone you trust
- Become educated about the disease
- Explain nature of illness to family members
- Be patient: the road is long
- Go to a meeting and get support
- AVOID preaching, punishing, providing excuses and protecting

And remember it is a treatable DISEASE.

CHAPTER 7

Betrayal

Integrity is based on our actions, not words or speeches we make, nor the guilt we might feel. One's character is judged by observable, consistent performances.

The Author

If I initiated a random dialogue and asked you the question "Has anyone ever done anything to you where you felt betrayed?", a proportionally high response would be "Yes". The "No" responders, in conducting their own survey, would predictably know friends, relatives or acquaintances that had been betrayed. The forms, severity and situations will be different as each version depends on the particular event where betrayal occurred and the time in one's life.

Veterans of longevity leash tirades against terrible actions far less often than those younger. With age comes acceptance. It is easy to underestimate the emotional imprint and invisible lacerations that lodge, germinate and are well-concealed. A fire drill of emotions — rage, hurt and sadness — can temporarily overpower a person during these transient flashes of recall.

In discussing this topic, the sources of the examples are from friends, associates and random stories revealed in passing. They are remarkably so similar to those of my patients that my audience would think they are from professional interactions. They are not, however, as the privacy and confidentiality of those who have sought my assistance is of paramount importance.

What I have learned is not the result of one mirror into anyone's life or of an advanced degree in spying. There are also no pretexts or halcyon delusions that we are all capable of justifying our own reprehensible actions.

The purpose of this chapter is to persuade the reader to think about behavior with a proactive mind set rather than cleaning up the mess retroactively. The underlying and overlying idea is to prevent the abdication of responsibility and to light up the blind spots in our perceptions. My aim is to confront these actions and barrage their disguises. It is my hope that it keeps a few people from falling into these tricky waters. We can interrupt the momentum of disarming behaviors that hurt others. Improving the album of living makes, perhaps, for a little nicer legacy.

It has been an intriguing inquiry into the subject of interpersonal betrayal. The lack of ethical decision-making occurs when one judges a behavior permissaable that has a high potential of harming another. Betrayal is an act or verbal statement that breaks some unstated, yet understood, code of behavior or moral arrangement between two people. Whatever word or description is used for betrayal, it connotes a transgression, a failure to conduct oneself in a generally moral way.

An assumption is made that if someone loves or respects us or is committed to us, he/she will not deceive us or commit an act that will harm. The code, when broken by either a bad decision or according to a calibrated plan, results in deception, which always erodes the trust between two people. A remedy for the offensive expedition must be generated in response or disintegration occurs. Even with some resolution, a tachardic trust remains, with one of the defendants vigilant for signs of another betrayal. And in some cases, trust is totally drowned in the floodgates of dishonorable actions.

Betrayers act in their own self-interest, from satisfying an impulsive need to a calculated form of deceit and hurt. When there is intentionality, rationalization is used in order to legitimize the act. This obliterates the unspoken or even articulated code of behavior between two people. There are times when impulsive behavior occurs especially in situations where excessive alcohol has been consumed. With a mushy conscience, they are provided with palliative excuses. As such, they feel they are disqualified from doing the "right thing."

When one is betrayed, it is a disorienting and painful experience. In order to obtain some emotional equilibrium, we partially blame ourselves. This analysis gauges the extent to which we were at fault and warranted the disastrous behavior. I am not referring to the minor reciprocal injuries tolerated in most relationships. One must, however, separate themselves from the judgment or belief that somehow they are responsible for the other's behavior.

It is the individual who does the betraying who is acting on his or her own rationalized projections. In some way, the betrayer might believe you have wronged them, which then justifies or minimizes his or her own actions. Betrayers have an efficiency of cognitions that condone their deplorable acts with a series of self-palliative justifications. Their shame, guilt and moral quotients are low at that time. Some betrayals are impulsive, yet many are planned with malevolent intent. In emphasis, it is the person who is consumed with rage, jealousy, hostility, egocentricity, or self-centeredness, accompanied by diluted moral and ethical internalized guidelines that diminishes the relationship. Interjected in this dynamic is a valence that is correlated with how much we are connected to that person. The closer we are emotionally, by blood, legal arrangements or friendship, the stronger the ability to mortify and confuse our views on loyalty and attachment.

Betrayal comes in many forms and exists in every microcosm and system in our society. Our leaders lie, commit crimes, harass, sexually exploit, bribe and then pretend to have integrity. Some have statistically improbable financial success, which most of the hardworking, or more honest citizens could never acquire — and then attribute it to luck.

There have been a thousand years of short stories and reservoirs of epics that depict the inauguration of individuals into the famous monuments of interpersonal lethality. There is a lacunae of right and wrong, a moral nihilism where many behaviors are generally acceptable. A vacuous space, a galaxy of excuses exists that include, "When is it my turn," "life's too short," or "I deserve it," ad nauseam. Self-revelatory disclosures on television, and in books and magazines, promote the idea that most anything is legitimate. We are becoming a society that watches and accepts anything in the moral arena, thus diminishing the viewer and the person involved in the actions.

People have become proficient at dissipating any offensive behavior. Some betrayals are more virulent than others, some take less lethal contours, but our threshold of acceptability is rising. In the context of a committed relationship (spouse, parent, friend) individuals have taken flight, given affection elsewhere, falsely accused, and in an amalgam of ways have caused irreparable damage. The summarizing list has been constructed either out of observation or a direct hit. Every reader could retrieve their own sources of events that has challenged one's equilibrium and trust in another.

In each of these domains are illustrations of actions where there is general agreement that they signify lapses of ethical judgment. Some are so obvious that it seems silly to enumerate them. Since they are done frequently however, it would be a moral failure to ignore them and chalk them up to "those things happen all the time." It is not meaningless to articulate what might be considered wrong, diminish in some small way its acceptability and offer alternatives. Readers can evaluate, apprehend consequences and make revisions using their own barometric index. The following anatomy of betrayal is subdivided into discrete categories as purely a function of simplification. I am also explicit in telling you that these are some of my biases when I assign a negative moral grade.

Sexual Offense (In and Out of Marriage)

- Husband having a sexual relationship with the best friend, sister, or co-worker of his wife or the reverse.
- A sister having sex with her sister's husband or boyfriend.
- Variations of the above theme.
- Any sexual act perpetrated on a child.
- Sexual exploitation of women or men.

Parenting Transgressions

- Emotional abuse.
- Not paying child support when you have the ability to.
- Replacing children from one marriage with those from a subsequent marriage.
- Selfishly spending money on yourself before your dependent children's needs.
- Using children to seek revenge.
- Choosing a man or woman over your children.
- Turning your children against your ex-spouse.
- Exploiting your children's trust.
- Dumping your children with other relatives or friends so you can have a good time.

- Not being responsible as a parent, the "Going off to find oneself" syndrome.
- Abandoning wife/children/husband.
- Not seeking psychological assistance when it is available.

Friendships and Family

- Suing a good friend.
- Malicious gossiping.
- Taking advantage of a friend.
- Undermining a friend's professional position or co-worker.
- Continual cancellations of agreed arrangements.
- Reneging on a loan.
- False accusations.
- Any calculating act of blatant self-interest that arbitrarily hurts another or demeans another.
- Trying to separate spouse from parents.

Marriage

- Abandoning a spouse due to his/her illness.
- Flagrant affairs.
- Abuse, neglect, violence.
- Demeaning, degrading behavior towards your spouse.

Hedging on Parenthood

When two people make a decision to become parents, by default or desire, there are certain non-reversible commitments that should be made and adhered to, barring holocaust events. The parents no longer come first and adults are expected to moderate their "personal" needs. At best, after many years, there will be a point in the non-ending timeline of parenting when eventually, there is some resemblance of equal time. Children need to acquire a sense of trust that only parents and extended family can create. Even if there are frequent disagreements, children learn that conflict may be inevitable, is sometimes solvable, yet, underneath this dissension, is a commitment to each other and the family. As parents, we are under an obligation, to assure safety, even if it goes against our self-interest.

Marriage and parenting are burdensome; yet it is the arena to resolve quarrels, share successes and failures and learn how to negotiate with others. Parenting is tedious and challenging. However, without continuous dual maintenance, children are always divided.

Parents must forfeit unrestrained freedom, and calculate a balance between everyone's demands. No parents should imitate Houdini and accomplish the perfect vanishing act. Renouncing parenthood is a small-scale crime, at the very least.

Gossip

"It is almost impossible to throw dirt on some-
one without getting a little on yourself."
Abigail Van Buren,
syndicated column (1991)

Although gossip is a natural occurrence, like floods and volcanoes and an obligatory ticket for acceptance into a group, it can also be a form of betrayal. While looking out the rear-view mirror as they try to get you in the back, gossipers tend to embellish their stories with acidic words or terse innuendoes, from mild abrasions to murderous deductions. These people are devoid of underlying concerns, like the fidelity of friendship, and present an occluded view of everyone's imperfections, the blackheads of the people they talk about behind their backs.

When divulging confidences, there is a distortion of the truth through both omissions and exaggerations. Certain aspects of damaging information can be magnified and selectively positioned so that it is out of context. Non-verbal gestures, using the eyes, hands and a mere shake of the head in a particular direction, can skew all the facts about a situation and position a statement.

Gossip tends to alleviate boredom, that everyday mundaneness that affects us all and gives the talkers and the listeners a sense of superiority, or self-righteousness. For some, it can mollify personal dissatisfactions. Gossipers set up decoys to entrap you with their questions and concerns. They are generally not self-revealing while enjoying the secrets you expose. These "G" individuals derive disturbing pleasure through the painful or secretive exposure of others. People who are satisfied with their lives, or who are so busy that they do not have the time or motivation to indulge in discussions that have malicious intent, are most likely to avoid the seductive trap gossip sets. Gossipers should warehouse their mental notes and supplant snooping with a dedication to enhancing their own life.

The Lethality of Money

Conflicts over money have blasted families to the opposite side of the continent. Money issues resonate in and out of family circumstances. Money is a quick way to induce carcinoma and can create serious emotional as well as physical illness within people.

Friends have related stories about a family member who cancels a debt because the lender has more money or the borrower is ill. The only person who should annul the loan is the one who gave you the money. Trusting you to repay a debt is the foundation of ethics and the lender's bank account is none of your business. Banks have more money than you do and they expect repayment no matter what the circumstances. If the negative events in your life require it, one can discuss the problem of repayment to ascertain if the loan can be changed into a gift.

Other offenses reside in the expectations of children as to the fairness of how much money each child receives. Favored children may be the recipients of monetary investments that confirm their specialness. That being the case, the risk is converting siblings into volatile adversaries. Money is the family bridge game where every member at or under the table keeps score. It is the lifeline to the larger issues of competition, love and approval.

Some families prescribe conditions for financial rewards. Control and punishment enact the power of money. In its most counterfeit form, it can be a vicious weapon and a reliable measurement of betrayal.

Causes of Betrayal

Considering the potential for harm from the aforementioned list and brief examples, the continual question arises "Why, and are there acceptable explanations for behavior that breaches forms of trust and safety that are a necessity for most relationships?" The question is not that easy to answer. There is something in me that even resists the notion that I can adequately add any revelation that hasn't dominated eras of philosophical inquiries.

In responding to this question I offer, obviously a diluted explanation, a reductionist extrapolation of a vast library of psychological causation. It would be ludicrous to presume that in a few paragraphs one can adequately narrow those predispositional factors that contribute to the mental states of individuals who harm others. In presenting summaries of extreme brevity, my aim is to add a little clarity to the etiology of betrayal and its countless permutations, not to excuse it. Nothing can fully account for the complexities that result in betrayals.

I am not referring to brief lapses of minor insensitivities, nor individuals with pervasive psychological disorders that have a paralyzing effect on the ability to perceive the correctness of actions. These elucidations are considered only in the spectrum of normal functioning of those of the mentally fully informed, although the division may be unclear, in the potency of the latter's actions.

It would be tempting to conclude that behavior is reducible to rigid categories of right/wrong, good/bad, or even demonstrate that there are categorical truths. Obliterating many pernicious actions is like sending a fed ex to Saturn. To state my concern: I am simply interested in thinking about decisions with a more reflective mindset and encourage the skill of moral discernment. To minimally contemplate doing the "right thing."

Causation is complex and determined by many factors. It may be rooted in family or individual history, the present emotional and physiological state, chronic or random. There are differences according to frequency, severity and intent. Although knowing right from wrong, certain precursors impede a person from making a decision that could avoid exceedingly negative consequences. I have confined this restrictive procrustean analysis to arbitrary categories that include: self-deception, narcissism, self-involvement, immaturity, deprivation and passivity. These categorizations may overlap, especially when individuals meet several of the criteria described. There is an elaborate mixture of strategies that can be generated to protect and justify the events we participate in. At times, we even take the emotional Concorde and retreat after our mistaken expeditions.

Self-deception

Each person nurtures illusions about themselves and others as a protection from anxiety and pain. This self-preservation aid is labeled denial. The word "denial" is an explanatory concept for occluded eyesight. Denial is the foundation of self-deception. It is the ability to ignore blatant evidence or hazy intuition about how we operate. Inveterate self-deceivers have immunological barriers that do not register sufficient guilt, or perception of cause and effect, which then prohibits sensitivity and awareness of others.

These individualistic mechanisms resist new or different information that might have the possibility of challenging a stance about oneself. In order to maintain adequate self-esteem, people convince themselves that they are correct or have the right to do what they are doing.

This self-bias helps us escape feelings of jealousy, abandonment and inadequacy by selectively focusing on what others have done, and excluding vital information about ourselves. In fact, blatant evidence presented by others does not diminish the fortress barriers we live in that confirm our views and legitimize other's culpability. Personal inquiries are avoided when denial is in full operation.

In order to process the complexities and contradictions of living, individuals need a cognitive map to clarify the struggles of living that makes accessible the various routes, back roads and multi-lane highways to arrive at the right place. Roadblocks must be intelligently navigated. There are many difficult junctures and detours where knowledge about oneself is a precondition to good judgment.

With regard to the necessary thought process, self-deceptors use a reductionist model. It is rigid, and filters out feedback from others. These blind spots, black holes of sight, give one permission to act carelessly. Unaware of their part or responsibility, they persuade themselves of their innocence, punctuated by smug indifference. It is a self-serving mechanism to edit, and re-edit their own history, which then protects against their vulnerability.

Ego-centricity-narcissism (Me and More Me)

While reading the characteristics of the self-centered individual, on the periphery of your thoughts might be friends, relatives or acquaintances. Ego-centrics obtain gratification by their intense need for chronic self-involvement and attention. This absorption dominates relationships and thus precludes a genuine interest in others. The quintessential definitions include synonyms of demanding, attention-seeking and indulgent. Everyone else is to blame for their problem, so they can justifiably take advantage or act against someone else. This translates into actions that revolve around competition and jealousy. There is an emotional fixedness, the distinct feeling that they are emotional cheerleaders, jocks, or somehow arrested in childish rebellion.

A genuine complexity and array of emotional depth is missing, resulting in a blandness. In some the girlish giggling, in order to ward off embarrassment, occurs frequently and at inappropriate times.

Binges of alcohol, random sexual activity, the interchangeability of impulsive craving and acting on it, catapult their partners into spasms of anger. Many men prefer golfing and hunting with their friends to fulfilling the requirements of being a partner or parent. They experience repetitive cycles for individualistic goals and pleasure. Decisions are essentially made for themselves, and they frequently overturn the rights of others regardless of prior obligations.

For these people, since rules are meant to be avoided or broken, actions are very impulsive. There is a regularity of over-indulgence with little remorse, and the pursuit of fun, gratification of any kind, is the "touchdown" of living. To reduce the risk of injury, the signal phrase "Hazardous Material" should be specified.

Immaturity

Immaturity is the failure to develop in the theoretically posited stages of growth. It can include a constricted conscience, a stunted ability to anticipate the consequences of one's actions and thought processes that are characterized by simplicity. Immature individuals have either limited experiences or minimally retrieve information from their present or past that generates learning that includes compassion, empathy and sensitivity toward others.

Immaturity is a misguided view of the world, a perceptual one-sidedness, almost blind to the complexity of life. Immature individuals take the first helicopter away from responding to life's demand and difficulties. They go in the opposite direction of responsibility and have perfected the stratagems for evasion. Everyone close to "maturity deficients" pays a debt for their actions.

A familiar encyclopedia of excuses have perpetuated and legitimized actions that are transparently full of potholes. It is the language of evasion; self-deception mediated by verbal habit. These statements corroborate one's tendencies towards selfishness and refusal to be accountable. Here are some that are probably familiar to you.

1. When is it my turn?
2. You only live once.
3. Children are resilient.
4. They don't need the money.
5. My problems are related to my low self-esteem or dysfunctional family.
6. I'm too old to change.
7. He/she or they deserve it.
8. I'm very expressive and can't control my emotions.
9. I need it.
10. Nobody's going to control me!

Doing the Right Thing

Many books and articles have been written focusing on forgiveness, getting over the hurts and continuous efforts to overcome pain caused by others. The harmed person has to construct a variety of methods to accept, forget, understand and/or put what they may not have even been deliberately part of, into an agreeable context. This chapter is not about that process. This is specifically for the person who has either intentionally or inadvertently done the wrong thing. It is more than holding a different point of view. To be mature requires the ability to take a hard look at one's actions or inactions and make amends commensurate with the severity of that neglect.

In many instances, each of us has chessboard of choices, each having different consequences. Life is an extensive multiple-choice exam. According to test construction experts, there are generally two wrong answers, one with shades of verity, and finally the best answer. We need to continually deliberate whether or not any given act is the right or wrong thing to do, and like a test, select the best choice. It is analogous to the two main ethical principles in medicine: beneficence and nonmaleficence. The first is to prevent harm or to act in the patient's best interest; the latter is to do no harm, in essence do not risk taking an action that will result in harm to another.

When you have done some action to someone else that is dishonest, revengeful, or extremely selfish, it only exacerbates the wrong to make lengthy explanations as to the causes and roots of your behavior. At times, these justifications only create more frustration and anger. There is an inference that some outside force or someone else shares in the blame. You have to acknowledge that you did something wrong, apologize and make amends in a way that is relevant to the injured party. It is your moral bank account, and is not shared by lovers, parents, your boss or any early childhood event. Barraging with excuses is unacceptable.

It is crucial that when you have harmed another, there is an emotional or moral debt that one has an obligation in some ways to meet. In most cases, the criteria for compensation is far less than the initial hurt. It is extremely difficult to balance out previous betrayals with present limited actions. The alternative, however, is nothing. These are duties of "reparation." Whether it ranges from just listening to the anger and hurt to financial compensation, something that demonstrates that you are prepared to remediate is essential.

We need to cultivate a view that behavior choices are voluntary and actions can be contemplated and evaluated. Defenselessness should be a rare exception more than a common practice. In a world of quick-fix gratification, the tolerance of discomfort is a significant individual challenge.

One might ask what are the ways that are conducive to producing the best possible outcomes. For brevity and avoidance of moral preaching, I have enumerated on a few. I simply suggest that the reader reflect on situations where choices are made that will require courage. Acts of omission may also be tantamount to betrayal. We are remiss in not intervening when situations occur that will benefit another. Passivity is also insidious. Withholding money, kindness or love are not neutral but as harmful as many other overt action that may seem more obvious in their consequences.

What follows is a list of suggestions to improve one's ability to engage in non hurtful behavior.

Betrayal Control Skills
- Defer actions - Deliberate.
- Discuss the situation with an impartial person.
- Formulate alternatives.
- Sublimate your immediate gratification needs.
- Contemplate the reverberating effects of a particular action on others.
- List the possible consequences of your actions.

- Define some rules: i.e., in parenting, your children should come first.
- Stop blaming everyone else.
- Recognize your early hurts and do something constructive about them.
- Deal with conflict without geysers of emotion.
- In decision-making, think of the worst case scenario.
- Evaluate and re-evaluate your actions.
- Try to recognize what part you played in a betrayal and acknowledge the wrongdoing.
- Listen to and look for input from valued friends.
- Fulfill promises.
- Choose truthfulness that inflicts little harm.
- Calm down, take time out and outwit your out-of-control emotions.
- Do not take advantage of others — do your part.
- Seek the counsel of individuals who will confront your distortions.
- Employ salutary humor before you resort to damage.

The Right Thing (Not Your Own Thing)

- How would you feel if this was done to you?
- What would you think about that person?
- What could be the worst outcome?
- What are the consequences of that outcome?
- How many people might be affected in a negative way?
- Do your motives originate from indulgence, jealousy, rebellion, defiance?
- If you retrieved your conscience, what would it tell you?
- How would an impartial spectator describe your actions?
- Are there other choices available?

CHAPTER 8

Marriage / Affairs / Divorce

One advantage of marriage, it seems to me, is that when you fall out of love with him, or he falls out of love with you, it keeps you together until you maybe fall in again.

Judith Viorst, in Redbook (1975)

A long-term marriage has to move beyond chemistry to compatibility, to friendship, to companionship. It is certainly not that passion disappears, but that it is conjoined with other ways of love.

Madeline L'Engle, Two-Part Invention (1988)

The very fact that we make such a to-do over golden weddings indicates our amazement at human endurance. The celebration is more in the nature of a reward for stamina.

Ilka Chase, Free Admission (1948)

If you are reading this chapter with the expectation that I have the answer to your marital condition, then I suggest you skip to divorce! Replicating the wisdom of the TV gurus who have given us convincing packaged formulas in their tapes, workshops and books is not my intent. There are enough experts who claim to fix, enrich, enhance, salvage, perform miracles, and intoxicate while promoting themselves to make money. Adding to your selection of solutions might cause unwarranted seizures. Relationships have been inspected, dissected and segmented to the tiny size of the mitochondria in the amoebae. It would be hard to name an enterprise that contributes more to the dramatic events in one's life. Post mortem inspection of marriages gone awry has revealed the probable causative disorders that have hastened the death of "the couple."

With digressions, this chapter suggests both actions and overall attitudes that couples have that seem to reduce the risk of drifting into divorce. There are, of course, the illusive and undefinable private and invisible "narcotics" that palliate some of the usual marital hurdles. They may be obsessions of one of the partners, loyalty, friendship, or a tight neurotic rope that permanently binds the couple. Marriage requires, though, a considerable sense of integrity that values the promises one makes to another.

There is also an avalanche of individually paid for commercial programs convincing the audience about the efficacy of their approaches to relationships. One of these marital mentors of the moment espouses the theory that we all have childhood wounds and should be committed to healing and "re-parenting" our spouses. Another, in a contradictory advertisement, specifically states, especially for women, "Do not mother your spouse." Resentment and rebellion will ensue. The latest convincing performance by an "expert" provides all the secret skills to relationships (after her four marriages!), but will reveal them only after you purchase her tape. The adage should be changed from:— "We learn from mistakes" to "we learn from what we did right."

Mixed messages are presented by the media. Some theorists encourage treatment that tells the individual to abandon the parasitic expectation that one should be nourished, comforted, and soothed by a spouse, and should give up the child's way of responding. This encourages autonomous development not based on some earlier deprivation. Others claim that couples should heal the wounds of each other's childhoods. Thus, someone else is giving you what makes you feel whole, better and complete.

Several marriage researchers believe that the seeds of relationships are planted in childhood, which germinate and flourish during adulthood, or are destroyed by early needs that go underwatered and are parched. The choices we make are unconscious, based on the early experience in our families. If you are confused by the unhappiness in your marriage, it has been suggested that you examine your past, the original site of the infection, and try to understand the distortions that might be influencing you. As a result of this historical dissection, we can then understand what causes you pain and anger, which leads to the rise of marital blood pressure. Genetic predispositions, like depression, can cause a decline in marital happiness manifested in progressive conflict, projections, frustrations, and then ultimately, its demise. The origin of our marital problems are inner convictions of associations to our family and the legacy it has given us.

Although many theories posit that the emotional development of adult-adult relationships are patterned by our given family, false deductions should not be made about the ingredients for success. We might misattribute good marriages to a salubrious childhood. I have known many couples whose histories are replete with "childhoods from hell." Their distinguishable events include alcoholism, or parents with manic-depressive illness, and emotional, financial and physical abandonment tendencies. As part of my social inquisitory manner, I've listened to many men who were subject to the Fascist school of discipline and Antarctic aloofness in their upbringing. And although these have been brief interactions, meaning: not living with them, several of these men are very sweet and kind and even sensitive. They also appear inordinately giving to their wives.

As couples, they are able to handle conflict with humor and civility. When one has lived with adversity, creating a better life may be comparatively less painful. Contrary to what one might believe, origination in families of relative stability and happiness does not necessarily give you a deposit on lasting marriage and vice versa. Yes, history does shape the present, but I reject the idea that as adults, this albatross has power over us. We can shed our parents' maladjustments. The link between the disturbances during childhood and adult characteristics are influenced by many mediating processes.

At a recent dinner, in one of those exclusive restaurants on Nantucket, with several past and present high-level corporate executives and their spouses, my husband and I were the only couple married once. When someone asked the secret of this accomplishment, in an impulsive, unguarded response, I narrowed the explanation to "Low Expectations." Everyone responded in laughter. My husband, believing he was rescuing me or himself, assuaged the moment by saying that it wasn't exactly what I meant.

It was. We have glorified, romanticized, fantasized, and infantalized marriage. There is a plethora of books about getting the love you want, addictive love, intimacy, communication, and relationship enhancement. Implicit in these offerings is that the focus of an existence together should be about what another person should give us because we deserve it, need it, demand it, as a way of compensation for prior injustices.

This concept may be the culprit that transports marriage into intensive care units: the thickets and thorns of great expectations. These fermenting ideas place a Herculean demand on another person whose weightlifting capacity may only be five to eight pounds! The marriage then gets catapulted into a pressure cooker with defective valves. In the early stages, myopic mania induced by the blindness of love screens out parts of our partners we might not want to see. Eventually, there are the normal lapses of perfection, the constant flow of need gratification, and the entire or real person appears, a true mirage. When we reach that place, we need to adjust, modify, and intercept the infantile clamoring of demands that results from reality intervening.

This is not to say that people cannot be emotionally or behaviorally responsive. It is the chronic flooding of demands, obsessive and/or intermittent, the "I need, I want, I expect, you never do this," the adnauseam complaints that have the Titanic affect of *"SINKING THE SHIP,"* and all aboard.

The success of marriage, as minimally measured by the absence of divorce, has been made more vulnerable by the persuasive appeal of the psychology of self. The paramount importance of meeting individual needs, a necessary requirement to be fulfilled in relationships, and compensation for what you didn't get as a child turns the functioning of the couple into the ubiquitous "me." This narcissistic bill of rights guarantees happiness, love, support, growth, fun, friendship, understanding, and empathy from the person we marry. More fallacious assumptions embedded in this doctrine are that there will also be sexual satisfaction, infused with excitement, romance and passion.

Marriage promises intimacy, great sex (sometimes on demand) companionship, friendship, fun, support, in short, a continent of fulfillment. Expectations also include fixing and healing the wounds of childhood, while fixing the clogged toilet. Unrealistic expectations are opportunistic infections; their growth depletes the entire organism. When one infrequently enrolls in the school of entitlement, failure can be avoided. Non-compliance in the syllabus results in projecting "Attila the Hun" qualities and motivations on our partners. We issue summonses that state: "He is selfish, demanding, controlling, distant, and uncommunicative."; "She is critical, never satisfied, not sexually responsive." Thus, the misleading malevolence oozes. The reasonable or functional view specifies that the less you need and want, the more potency you add to the longevity of the relationship, modifying the discontent. A course in criticism should not be taken.

Another marriage potion is the ability to tolerate anger, disappointment and other emotional compulsions without globalizing into a nuclear disaster. This would include the Red Cross Therapy of not escalating all the differences and conflicts. The agile waverunners ride the currents instead of fighting and ultimately drowning. These emotional navigation abilities generally indicate a maturity that avoids arrival into dangerous territory. For many couples, it is easy to sink into the quicksand of accusations and screaming epithets. Generally, one of the duo brings the other one into the mire with them. It's how we negotiate the same problems.

There are individuals who believe that expressing one's feelings, venting, indulging in hysterics, the high Richter scale of catharsis, is generally good for a marriage, a.k.a. "The getting-it-off your-chest" solution. It may be a relief for the party engaged in this adolescent solution. However, after the infantile clamoring tantrum is over, this explosion creates agitation in the other party. If a bomb were ticking loudly, and you knew it was going to detonate, fleeing would be the safest response. So it is with marriage. The person connected to you during the high-voltage activity is feeling as though he or she is looking over a cliff with agoraphobia, trapped in a paralytic position, and is unable to move or react. Nuclear fission is a lousy communication style.

The smart member of the marriage duo relinquishes the self-intoxicating approach of violent interaction and regulates the dosage, reducing the high volume of recurring screeching and taking the track of sensible detours. Words of hostile intensity never helped and in fact, increase the risk for coronary marriage disease.

There are also the recurrent practical problems related to the division of expected labor and competency. Many couples are in the business of requesting plastic surgery on each other. One is always trying to make the spouse into something they never were: the klutz into a handyman, the silent reticent into an intense interactor, the man with a barracuda-like mean streak into a guppy. When you expect something that was never there, or only present in bits and pieces, trouble is ahead.

Different Kinds of Marriages

There are many kinds of marriages with varying degrees of temperamental intensity. The fiery, combustible combinations appear like trajectories, sliding on black ice, spinning out of control. They, however, may be well-suited in their love of drama, turmoil and subsequent passion. The magnetic intoxication of opposites is the wild west version of staying together.

Other couples are more monotone or placid, like a still lake. They would be miserable in an ECT (Electric Charge Therapy) marital style. They are not particularly bored or dissatisfied. The importance of emotional quietness is what works for them. "On the fulcrum" type of relationships combine several elements. There is a mix of calmness with surprise sandstorms.

There are couples where both place a high value on independence and would feel choked with arrangements that required constant closeness. They value separateness and bring differences to the relationship. Others are far more comfortable with frequent togetherness in their daily routines and additional activities.

The art of dance is a good analogy to the beauty of different forms of marriage. The fox trot couples like to work together, respond to the rhythms of their partner, and have to be attuned to the steps and the nuances, like the timing of the synchronized swimmers. Drama, intensity and passion characterize the tango couples. Others like to dance physically apart, country line formations, content in their individual expression — distance between them, yet connected.

What Makes Marriages Work

Successful and satisfying marriages do exist. The prevailing standards differ as much as cloud formations. Under microscopic viewing, however, the elements of success appear clearer. Marriage is about couples eventually developing a moral sense, rather preachy terminology. This is not sentimentality. It is based on consideration of someone else. The relationship evolves into something that is unmistakably fair to both partners.

Marriage requires a restructuring of personal needs and of narcissistic involvement. Individual freedom may not be the central focus anymore. Self-serving hedonism is sent permanently to the cleaners. Indulging oneself in things that your family may not be able to afford, or ignoring how the priorities of these resources may be needed in the future, is selfish. The narcissist in the marriage can be the major destroyer. For conflict avoidance there should be some agreement on the allocation of finances, child-raising if there are any, and general value similarity. Morality is connected to control.

In most vintage relationships, romance has been replanted by accomplishing things together and the capacity to take action that will turn off the "red alert" alarm clock. Although there may be different and opposing individual views, the attitude overall is a desire to get through the obstacles in an effective way.

As all relationships will travel through phases and changes, it is vital to be able to tolerate these seasonal fluctuations. In many good marriages, there is far less emphasis on sex. During the course of a satisfying marriage, the pharmacy of companionship supplements the previous stages of intensity. The pleasure and positive aspects are very different, as the relationship progresses, from the early epileptic seizures to a newly formed couple and ultimately arriving at stability and satisfaction.

Not surprisingly, compromise is a "careful and well-constructed" way to accommodate differences. This reconciling by "giving in" or giving up some things is a prelude to avoiding hostilities. Wanting to win or getting your own way is interpersonally detrimental. The mechanism underlying compromise is less like losing and more like the stock market: an investment in the near and distant future, and the beneficial outcome of controlling our childish self-centered focus. Individuals who have an overdeveloped sense of "I" need explicit training in compromise. Other couples enrich their marriage by sharing individual goals, pleasures and interests. They accept the other's limitations so that they are not frequently disappointed.

Editing your words, considering your actions, and keeping your own thoughts in your inner personal vault break the endless cycles of chronic indigestion that couples give themselves. The "marriage patrol" is sending out summonses to anyone who continually acts out their own self-centered dramas. Learning to ignore the small things broadcasts maturity.

Couples that report marital satisfaction try to see the other person's point of view or perceptions and are able to articulate them. Minimally trying to understand someone's feelings or thought process creates an atmosphere or communicates to the other person that someone is at least trying and cares enough about you in that attempt. This does not mean agreeing with adoring enthusiasm. Marriage does not necessarily have to be a quid pro quo to equalize every facet of giving and taking. Perhaps, although immeasurable to the naked eye, it appears that one is giving more or is at the opposite side of the taking net. The general idea is to give naturally and thus improve the relationship.

Individuals must learn how to endure the lousy weather, the periodic cold spells, and even the frigid tundra. With time and patience, relationships generally move to more bearable circumstances. Part of that slow marathon is the belief that things will get better. Less impulsivity is the way to avoid the potholes. The partners have the ability to distract themselves or have outlets in preparation to their partner's foul-weather mood. The "this will pass" solution, instead of issuing "global warnings," prevents unnecessary slides into lava. Testosterone flare-ups flame out quickly when left unfueled.

Marriage and Money

It may not be the root of all evil, but it can give the marriage a real toothache. The context of disagreements about the "M" word have multiple meanings and challenges, and may require "root-canal" work. Money is a synthesis of multiple meanings, including: altruism, control, individuality, independence, fairness, family history, manipulation, retaliation, selfishness, and hopefully, love and kindness.

Besides the overt manifestation in the deployment of marital funds, there are subtexts of personal agendas of which the couple may not even be cognizant. There is an array of interactional patterns that emerges or slowly develops. If one of the spouses is indulgent and wants everything either for his or her own gratification or for perceived status, the other has to compensate by being frugal, being a nag, or existing in a state of anxiety. The spender has a sense of entitlement or deservedness, and he (and I will use this pronoun as I am thinking of a particu-

lar male) sees his core identity as based on his acquisitions —
the bigger, the more prestigious, the better he temporarily feels.
The marital duel emerges: the Spartan verses the Hedonist.

Another dominating condition that creates dissension and
chronic unhappiness is spousal control of partners through
money. The money earner, if there is only one, assumes a superior architectural identity, and controls the resource allocations.
The unequal partner is more dependent and has less
decision-making authority. If money is used as a tool for power,
the currency control devalues the one not holding the green
cards. This is a perilous dynamic. Men generally retain this power
in marital relationships.

A typical means of undermining a relationship is to spend
money excessively, in a mode of retribution or in a self-consumed
importance. When perennial conflicts in other areas of the marriage are not negotiated or solved, getting even by overspending
is the self-justifying recourse of one or both of the marriage
partners. Getting back by selecting the bankruptcy model of
revenge is taking the wrong road sign. It debilitates the marriage
and is potentially dangerous. It temporarily feels like power and
it looks like assertiveness; but unchecked, it's as lethal as intra-
venous drug binges. Purchasing symbolic ornaments that provide
status in the relationship perpetuates mini-crises and possible
long-term financial problems. Money is a conduit to our psyches — perhaps more evident than sex. Individuals who feel
cheated in their lives, either by love or attention, compensate
by filling up the emptiness and hurt in the things they acquire.
Our economic society encourages and idolizes objects of afflu-
ence. Acquisitions are related to feelings of competency, worth
and entitlement.

The ideal solution is a mixed recipe with variations and
creativity in the ingredients. A normal curve of distribution, a
statistical tool that assumes in the middle section are the pooled
resources that are allocated for consistent expenditures. The tails,

as they are called, are the individual and personal waterfalls. Each can fill in their own equations.

A simple formula to consider is as follows: If joint income is $70,000, expenses and savings $60,000, then each partner has discretionary income of $5,000. Inheritances belong to the inheritor as it was never a joint venture.

Financial management is only one facet of the couple's ability to adapt to the evolution of a long relationship. When spouses are not equals, they have a pattern of relating with a "high risk" index.

Challenging Marriage Partners

There are a group of individuals with an abundance of psychologically negative bank accounts that they are unable to relinquish. These dispositions require intensive intervention, a messianic psychological conversion. If you are married to such a person, it is best to accept the chronic flare-ups and the infrequent remissions.

These individuals include the narcissists whose vocation is to reside in the center of the solar system. Their performances require consistent attention. The rings of Saturn surround them so that initially they appear seductive and exciting. All the board games have to move in their direction. Much of this kind of marriage is one of immense energy invested in idealizing, paying attention and living with frequent emotional fluctuations.

A close relative to the narcissist is the notable person who lives by The Declaration of Independence: his or her right to enjoy themselves in the pursuit of happiness. Golf, hunting, fishing, going out with friends, obsessions with activities outside of the marriage, is an operational given. Having time restraints or expected obligations are a challenge with individuals harboring this interpersonal orientation. They are not inclined to participate fully in household or domestic requirements.

Whenever we think of marriage, the association with passion, intimacy and close connections appear in our parables of love. However, this field of vision is an ulcerous condition for a specific style of relating. Certain individuals do not find comfort in closeness. The traits that characterize their functioning are more dispassionate; they strike their interior balance with an extraordinary need for solitary pursuits. They are not particularly self-revelatory, and their native language is not "feelings." In battles, "retreat" is their chosen maneuver. Self-sufficiency is essential and demands from others for intimacy are viewed as tyrannical.

I doubt if I could enumerate all the dispositions of the generic nature of all married people. There are the adventurers, dreamers, authoritarians, the passives, accompanied by the aggressors. In the long and short marriage Olympics, it is easier to circumnavigate the dispositions of the gods and then softly encourage them to contemplate change.

Marriage and Children

There will be a stampede of disagreement and opposition to the argument that responsible parents should employ every strategy to stay married. I can hear the rumblings, the individual hostile revolutions, that forcibly require two people who believe they are incompatible or hostile to "live together for the sake of children." To reduce the guilt and justify our actions, many claim that a bad marriage does not benefit, and often damages, the children. It is still large-scale gambling to dance, stumble or slither away from the dual-coordination of taking adequate care of and honoring an obligation to children, a fundamental loyalty. Parenting is not a part time, every other weekend job. That's irregular maintenance.

Parents transmit all types of free-falling attitudes, especially how indispensable and important they are as parents and thus, how much they value the children. In remaining together, even during the turbulent events, children learn that arguing, tensions, fights and retreats, may lead to some problem-solving or at least periods of suppression of a hyperactive cycle of exaggerated and adrenalin induced responses. These repetitive patterns are at least predictable and even appear to show some commitment to the resolution of differences or burial, or the intertwinement of both. Perseverance under fire is the test of integrity.

I certainly do not deny the realities of the overwhelming unbearable feelings when a marriage is in a difficult place, as if one is shipwrecked with constant seasickness. The anger and rage are so powerful; the other person is often wished dead. Or the degrees may be as a low-grade, unremitting marital infection.

Conflict is fatiguing. The retreat from the battleground of recriminations, the same uncomfortable torment, overpower the couple. Pent up mutual sneering and disdain develops instantaneously, signaling another emergency. Some spouses entertain fantasies of escape or rescue. One can be incredibly alone, an orphan, yet supposedly related in marriage. There is that acid disconnection and the realization that the fit is difficult.

We all develop strategies away from the unpleasantness. Hopefully, there is comfort in children, a job, friends, and not in a substance of abuse or on other destructive roads. Cautiously, the spouses weave back towards each other. The episodes repeat, with variations. Marriage can be unpleasant, adversarial or just tolerable.

In staying together, children, especially older ones, learn that differences, disillusionment, frustration, communication failures, hurt and anger, enacted in these episodic flurries, may not be considered terminal events. When parents continually work toward a resolution, albeit dyspeptic, it reflects the value that the family and children are important. Coupling is for the resilient, malleable and those who are a little masochistic. The model of marriage longevity may be a little diseased, but at least there is something to emulate.

Statements of rationalization — "I raised my children and now it is my turn," or "I waited until my children were out of school" — should generate acclaim for decency. If marital partners stay until a specific celebratory event, it implies that liberation and independence should be forgiven. What is the deciding age? Elementary school, college? What are the specific markers that assure one that the damage will be minimal? These slogans of self-actualization, autonomy, and freedom above required obligations are the high-rise rhetoric that generally cowers above selfishness.

I've also heard nauseating stories about exits from a marriage. One gentleman announced at his daughter's wedding that he was leaving his wife, the mother of the bride. Perhaps he envisioned a dual celebration. Soon after her husband's diagnosis of MS, a wife demanded a divorce. A doctor serially marries and divorces his nurses; the search for the perfect RN.

One comment of dubious merit is that children in divorce situations have been most supportive and understanding of their divorcing parents. This is not a decision of multiple options: children in the divorce crises are limited to begging, crying, manipulation, and hospitalizations as their possible reactions. Balancing both sides lessens the chances of being abandoned; agreement which sometimes translates into "support" is their only option. AWOL IS AWOL: defection exemplifies a permissive view of promise-keeping. It is primarily for the adults.

I personally dislike sermonettes and proffered advice, but I believe we serve our children poorly by leaving a marriage. They inherit cynicism towards relationships. Young adults' pictures of the future are fragmented with fear and doubts about relationships, a jaundiced view. The impact of divorce is a lifelong weight which exhibits itself differently at various life-stages. There is ample evidence to prove the children get caught in the divorce fugue of financial revenge and spousal punishment.

As applied to parenting: "Character is the enduring and consistent influence, a lifelong series of actions, that our children can emulate. It is a distinctive conglomeration of behavioral and ethical-decisions that are re-enacted daily and bypass the words we elicit." In short, actions speak louder than words.

Marriage is a process of transformation. An alliance that has new challenges at various intersections. There will also be disappointments because of the differences between people that result in difficulties of living together. It is important to recognize that any relationship has its intense dissatisfactions and overwhelming demands. There are however, some strategies that can minimize the chronic turbulence, gatekeep, and improve the quality of the marriage. It is my hope that the following list stimulates your own thinking and provides some benefit to couples.

Twenty-one Propositions About Marriage

1. Do not take your partner hostage by asking or expecting too much.

2. The less you blame your partner, the more you can solve your marital problems.

3. Screaming louder, longer and with added cruelty will result in deaf ears.

4. There are generally explanations for behavior that one attributes to malevolence.

5. Couples may have to adopt new rules for marriage.

6. Misinterpretation occurs all the time. No event is seen the same by two people.

7. A single affair, or "one-night stand," is not enough to be branded as unfaithful.

8. For some, a good prescription might be a brief sabbatical, time out or frequent intermissions, maybe separate quarters.

9. You only have to work hard on relationships that require hard work.

10. Power issues in relationships are generally about money, sex and division of labor.

11. Leave character assassinations for the terrorists.

12. There is no need to express all the time what you are thinking and feeling. It should be selective and well-timed. (In other words, exercise silence and self-control).

13. Marriage is all about expectations. They should be realistic and accommodating.

14. Marriage is cyclical and cyclonic. Coast through the storms—preservers are plentiful.

15. Vent your frustrations to a friend.

16. Find humor in your own behavior and your spouse's. (It's easy.)

17. Don't ask for or demand what you can't get.

18. The marriage loses when one partner has to win an argument.

19. As in anything we do well, marriage is interesting work and a lifelong commitment.

20. Remember, you exchange one set of problems for an other.

21. If you can give it, why not! (material things and positive emotional affect: praise, appreciation, empathy)

Affairs, Extra-Marital Relations, Infidelities

From one projection screen to the next, affairs are in the forefront of our viewing. Princesses and presidents, commoners and congressmen are the public actors in the "coming attractions." The publicity and ratings rival any war in a beleaguered country and easily bury any social issue on the scene at one time. Audiences respond with a mixture of curiosity, voyeurism and fascination. It allows the capacity for judgment and criticism. As an outcome, individuals can airbrush their own lives equivalent to reconstructing superiority. Leadership infidelity is a rather pathetic advancement that the public is subjected to willingly. Simultaneously, the spouse of the person having the affair seems to avoid the target of blame and resembles Joan or "John" of Arc.

There are many explanations for the occurrences of the breaking of traditional marital agreements and the numerous casualties that occur in the fallout. It includes some unmet needs, unreasonable expectations, a pattern of behavior that existed prior to marriage, and in its early development, an avenue to accommodate to difficulties in a marriage. Society, at present, emphasizes self-development and "self" gratification. Some individuals have ego difficulties, requiring inordinate amounts of attention. Others have high excitement quotients; they like to take personal risks and are easily bored. One of the most common spectrums of personality conditions is the one that covers the range of characteristics of those who are primarily emotionally immature, impulsive, or need some relief from inner discomfort or torment; characteristics that are the embodiment of addiction.

Infidelity comes in many forms, from one discrete, unintentional event to a compulsive, ego bolstering series of disattached encounters. It may or may not be a repudiation of the spouse, depending on pre-existing determinants and circumstances, prior patterns of intense excitement, narcissism, high adventurism, preferences, and rule breaking.

Intrinsic in the affair is secrecy, romance, an idealized image of love, and an intense focus on the two participants. A loss of self may occur with an obsessional force toward the romantic, sometimes a sexual quality: the perfect oceanic merging. The topography is not repelled or cluttered by laundry, dishes, taxes, decisions, in-laws, or the neatness-sloppiness dimension. Encapsulated time zones of the couple create an immunity from the peculiarities and difficulties of married life. Many therapists believe some or all affairs are the result of some disturbed dynamic within the marital relationship itself. I tend not to agree fully with that theory. Affairs may be symptomatic of some problems in the relationship or may originate within the individual. Certainly, individuals with dramatic tendencies need to be continuously reaffirmed, and generally, validation by their spouses does not fill up the void.

Marriage to the same person, may just be tiring, with the same problems, explosions and misunderstandings. Many times in an asymmetrical event, one of the individuals silently contemplates leaving, with an outside force pressuring, lightly or vehemently. When the third party softly coaxes or pressures the spouse to leave, they are then blamed for the demolishment of the relationship. There may be evidence, however, that the marriage was already dead and the lover filled the role as undertaker. Affairs that precipitate the dissolution of a marriage may or may not result in remarriage. The new relationship may flame out or carry different problems and result in another divorce.

Affairs that last a long time require lying, planning, and secretiveness, which often adds to the excitement. The one having the affair may feel guilty about these actions. It may make the person look like a good spouse. But, for some, there is a constant internal comparison, in which one member appears deficient. The faithful spouse is blind to the competition and is running a race handicapped. Some affairs are strictly train tickets to leaving and they, in themselves, are not the cause of the break-up.

Generally, men react much worse to a wife's affair — it was never their fault, they say, while obsessing, blaming and remaining in paralyzed rage. A condition of powerlessness, their perception of a lack of control over their marriage tends to expose men's illusions about themselves. As men's roles may be organized around competition and possessiveness, they are inexorably disturbed by the threat to their self-definition. In gender-related reactions to affairs, men initially isolate themselves and thus have more inhibitions about resolving the distress by talking openly with friends.

In order to overcome the damage to a marriage, both members of the couple should attempt a better understanding of the event, stop to bury fossilized thoughts about the guilty party, and use this difficult situation to reconstruct their marriage. Fidelity is only one of several agreements we make, and the others we have smashed along the way are just as important.

When we examine the motivations that may account for an affair, an archipelago of scenes occur. An essential concept is that there are divergent reasons for a particular behavior.

To short-circuit the endless cycle of affair recriminations, defenses, tears, blaming, and rage, I have often thought of presenting the couple with a guilty-party decree. They could jointly decide on the length of punishments, the type, method, and what behaviors would be required for parole. The warden, of course, would be the spouse who had been monogamous and could supervise their spouse's probation. It would save a lot of money and time in therapy.

Punishment Time for Extra-Marital Affairs

Types & Severity	Punishment (Months/Years)	Method
One-night stands	1-6 months	Behaviors
Brief encounters (1-3X)	3-8 months	required
Long-term (1-3 years)	1-1 1/2 years	for parole
Affairs with close friends*	1-3 years	The judge would decide.

*No parole

The Punishment Infliction Schedule is a solution for the self-righteous partner. Although this proposal is suggested with a humorous implication, the management of the post-affair crises is riddled with blame. There may be no intention of humiliating or hurting the spouse. Society, with its highly sexualized features, may play an important role in influencing affairs. The proposal should be made for a no-fault affair.

Destination: Divorce

When feuding couples enter my office, the war maneuvers have already begun. Each person has a position, and the repetitive rounds of frustrations, losses, and damages re-occur, ignited instantaneously. These negative tactics appear in various forms. A dose of agent orange occurs when one of the spouses intermittently threatens divorce. This Kamikaze routine undermines the other's efforts and does not augur well as a prognosis for the future. Each party has a stockpile of weapons.

Increasing the decibels of one's voice, in order to punish or be heard, is a symbolic representation that the other has been deaf. It does seem strange that these incendiary castigations are an attempt to ameliorate the hurt or provide some temporary relief. Does inflicting pain or guilt, being self-righteous, using money as a weapon or other instinctual forms of self-preservation, have any other gain but sailing into an Antarctic impasse? Further down the evacuation may be necessary.

In the development of any relationship, an array of projections emerge that are believed characteristic of the spouse. Then to solidify these attributions, we analyze what these behaviors mean. These interpretations generally have malevolent, negative, or critical components. Seldom are these interpretations totally correct. No one can be sure of another person's motives, considering we don't even understand our own. Behaviors are automatic and multi-dimensional. We also have a propensity, due to our limited logic, to reject evidence that one does not want to admit. The couple is in white-capped waters, intent on insulting one another, and it has developed advanced expertise in verbal killing. On the horizon, selfishness and control appear representing our assailing bias.

Resentments and projections occur when we have expectations that the other person will satisfy some specific need, and with remarkable fervor, presumptuously believe that we are entitled to this satisfaction. We need to rewrite the formulas for marriage to include a "needs reduction" formula. Marriage is not magic, it's not what we believe we deserve, nor is it an emotional spa. It requires resilience and heroic dedication.

Divorce

> *A divorce is like an amputation; you survive,*
> *but there's less of you.*
>
> Margaret Atwood, in Time (1973)

> *Divorce is the one human tragedy that reduces*
> *everything to cash.*
>
> Rita May Brown, Sudden Death (1983)

> *So many persons think divorce a panacea for*
> *every ill, find out, when they try it, that the*
> *remedy is worse than the disease.*
>
> Dorothy Dix, in Dorothy Dix, Her Book (1926)

In general, divorce is a perpetual losing battle; a surface litigation over property, support, children, alimony and sometimes the perceived "other" woman and man variable. Divorce can mimic a terrible marriage, as a polypathetic event. Since each person gets half, it's never enough, no matter how much or how little there was.

Under the surface is a sinkhole of emotions and thoughts that do not inspire Good Samaritan transactions. The subterranean tides may fester with rejection and rage, sprinkled with a little vindictiveness. Most are sorrowful with an undercurrent of disappointments, depression and sadness. There is a need to reclaim power and control.

Leaving a relationship can be a way of alleviating some tension or disappointment about or within oneself or the marriage. This temporary reprieve, like a cancer in remission, can be delusionally freeing. When there is a personal malaise, or we are at odds with ourselves, moving on or out appears a salutary solution. This interpersonal discomfort drives us to the closest interstate, and we desert our family.

However, there is also a strong tendency to repeat past performances, thus exchanging one spouse for another. Your personal compass will pull you toward a person very similar to who you originally married. It is remarkable how different-appearing people turn into an identical twin in temperament, reactivity and interests.

For men, particularly, in our hypersexual saturated environment, another relationship rejuvenates their sagging identity. Entitlement and admiration of others persuade men to replace old wives and enhance their egos with younger and attractive spouses.

Often central to the marriage-deserter's thinking is that the other spouse is the culprit who, like Hercules, should shoulder all the blame. All the injunctions are rooted in psychological entitlement. The lawsuit claims that: "I have been unhappy for years because of you." Some divorce practitioners, stubbornly, like adhesive, believe that the dissolution of their marriage is a result of the bad angles of the other person. They blame and assign a master card of charges in numerous dimensions: malevolence, low intelligence, inadequacy, sexual dysfunction, selfishness, not meeting my needs. These projections shift and pamper the accuser and warp his or her ability to be introspective. Unfortunately, discrediting a spouse vetoes an opportunity for self-understanding.

No one has a clean mirror to gaze into. Divorce or the contemplation of the exodus from marriage should require that both individuals take an inventory of their own limitations, try to measure themselves more, and understand their contributions. Immaturity, fixated narcissism, and abandonment of responsibility are recognizable by the clichés: "When is it my turn?"; "The children will be fine."; "I stayed until they were in college."; and a maze of alternative explanations that are self-confirming rhetoric which immunizes one from the truth.

In leaving, we often deceive ourselves and others with a psychological lexicon of rationalizations. We've become a society that is entitled to freedom; we feel a psychological necessity to refurbish our lives and psyches — to make a declaration of "Personal Renewal." Individuals want reassurances and verification that their decision for future happiness and pleasure is a right freely exercised. New opportunities and inner transformation are found via divorce and certainly not in marriage, and if the children are in trouble, you can always send them to counseling, or so people tell themselves.

Divorce is about virtually everything: morals or missing morals, revenge, betrayal, lies, and the suffering of children. To justify actions, scapegoats are invented: In-laws and friends, and spouses subscribe to the concept that marriage is not a healthy institution; divorce is a normal meteorological problem, a natural force of nature.

Some individuals in the divorce marathon stoop low. A prior neighbor of mine, a relatively affluent man, during the separation period, stole half of the spices in their kitchen during his wife's absence. I assume he took the saffron, the most expensive. This act seemed to reflect a particular form of animosity due to her interest in cooking. As a side dish, he had left her for the woman next door.

I am certainly not suggesting that anyone stay in a marriage of abuse, cruelty, rampant destructive alcoholism, or irreversible misery. Traumatic marriages need dramatic exits, either carefully or quickly. This is not an argument against all divorce nor a nostalgic illusion of harmonious living, nor do I think that divorce should be a vilified event.

In some cases, I have seen marriages in such destructive states, spouses showing years of such ravage on each other, that divorce is probably the best solution. Yet, many times, I see one of the partners so self-centered and motivated by one's own needs, that he or she wants to be in another relationship and chooses their own happiness instead of their children's or spouse's. Many of the spouses who leave for another person may be happier. However, some choose to fulfill the obligation and responsibility of a parent and stay. The liquidation format allows so much social tolerance for the new woman or another man in the child's life. In the many years of couple observation, marital interruption, and ending because "one fell in love with another woman," is predicated on the mental split between what is "good for me or better for my family." Rationalizations about that decision can fill up a bathtub. These relationships were not particularly unhappy.

The comments that permeate this chapter are concerned primarily with defaulting on duties toward children. Inflicting guilt is not my intent. Rather it is an expression of concern for the inherent ethical decisions in divorce, primarily when there are children. Promise-keeping is discarded too easily, into bins of self-serving debris. I maintain it is reflective of the individual and not the institution. There are harmful consequences to the idea that individual happiness supersedes the commitments we need to make for our children. This collective mythology is a misguided vision that adults come first. From the point of view of the children, it is counterintuitive to assume that after the tidal wave of changes divorce brings, the children will adjust and be more resilient as adults.

Divorce, for the most part, is for the convenience of adults, with mixed legacies for the children. Parents produce selective evidence that the children will be happier with parents who live separately. The fallacy in this thinking is that parents assume that the underpinning of their children's daily lives are directly connected to their own sense of joy, pleasure and contentment. Children are more egotistical and self-centered, however, as they should be. Divorce removes the focus from the children to the adults.

Protracted litigation can injure children. Spasmodic fighting with mounting grievances drain spouses emotionally and physically, which decreases the stamina they need to deal with children. If you believe that divorce will have a minimal affect on your children, you are deceiving yourself. Approximately 50% of ex-spouses are angry at the divorced other, which does not dissipate for years, if ever. Medea's temperament — the revenge and rage — continue over lifespans. Do not delude yourself by thinking that therapy will ameliorate the pain and suffering of your children.

Divorce brings so many permutations in these children's lives — step-parents, blended families, half-siblings — that each child's history looks like that of the kings and queens of England. George the second, Henry the first; it is the "Fed-Ex" era for children. We pack them up, ship them on buses, trains, planes, and car shuttles. One could say it prepares them for employment in the postal-service industry. Other parents shed children like trinkets. They slow down their appearances in the child's life and their attendance at events, and finally altogether, a no-show in every way.

Raising children requires as many hands, hearts, financial and emotional resources as two parents can give full-time. Shared parenting is never half. What I have seen, though not in all cases, is that the parent who has left also leaves the daily chores, the daily guidance, the homework and endless obligations. The parent on call 24-hours gets very little relief.

Children need a complete family, including a father. Both parents provide structure, consistency and different ways to solve problems. Only about one or two out of ten children are relieved about a divorce. In the divorce chess game, the children lose. They are no palliatives. Time doesn't heal all wounds. When you separate and then divorce, there are several inferential messages that are transmitted by "satellite" to your children. One is that nothing lasts, so be cautious. Most children of divorce do not have a sense of permanence. Commitment is variable and can be transferred to a relationship with another person. In the view of these children, mothers and fathers can be replaced. When there is another person in the divorce equation, the conflict of allegiances occurs for children of all ages.

Children always pay the price for their parents' fallibility. If you look closely enough, you'll see the pain; it is impossible to disguise. Listen intently and hear the signs of distrust and pessimism. Their inheritance is fear that they will re-enact the marriage failure. It is adversarial to children's lives as they have to cope with an insecure tableaux, a great divide of loyalty, adjusting and readjusting to the chess players of lovers, kings, queens, and young knights.

There is also uncertainty about their parents' individual futures, the dating and step formations (stepparents, siblings, grandparents, aunts); the interchangeable steps are not country line dancing. A variety of responses to the evolving environment is reflected in depression, acting-out behavior, and even being "too" good, an extreme direction for success (or failure). I may be on fragile ground, but staying together for the children's sake can be considered an altruistic deed.

While the weather during divorce prosecutions can be raw, the post-finality climate can be an arctic tundra walk. There are some couples that let the ice-caps melt and retain civility for the children. All this prolific "good divorce" literature may theoretically sound good, but if the couple did not have the skills during the marriage, how will they act during and post-divorce? Does it sound like "for the children?"

Each divorce is a trial morality play. In the civil action against each other, the plaintiffs lose something. Only the lawyers gain — money. Generally and statistically, fathers slowly disappear. As most do not have custody, they exit and enter, weaving a dispensable potholder. Their ability to assert authority is minimized. The hourly and daily linkages rust and sever. Although some fathers have incredible talent at trying to climb over hurdles, and frequently leap tall buildings, co-parenting is a relentless challenge. There is a slow drifting away, a diminished capacity to influence, and in many cases, visiting becomes erratic and infrequent.

Of all the divorces I have witnessed outside my office, most were attributed to the enterprise of substituting one relationship for another. The break-up of the marriage was precipitated by an affair. Others left because "they fell out of love" or were bored — "freedom" fighters determining their personal course. None of them, as far as my telescope could see, had marked controversy or raging conflicts, nor irreversible damage. Primarily, the divorce stemmed from the men's malaise and in fewer cases, the women's.

This ends my compulsion to in some way cultivate capacities that reside in most people. These moralistic stands are not offered because of any self-righteous behavior, as I have been capable of actions that I would gladly delete from my obituary. Nor do I adhere to the idea that members of the media and politicians performing slogans that extol family values should be listened to as many of them have divorced for their own personal pleasures.

My prejudices and judgment should be taken with caution as I even am suspicious of experts whose own lives have morals easily sucked up in vacuum cleaners. Dispensing advise, even from professionals, is arguably a pompous act. Some parts of this narrative may not win the reader's approval, and if you're divorced, you won't like what you've just read.

Perhaps resurrecting altruism, commitment, consistency, loyalty, and sacrifice for family, are not exactly soap-opera activation. A pendulum reversal is needed to legitimize the message that children are more important than adults, and to dismiss that concept is negligent. At minimum, decreasing the divorce rate should be in our family-business forecast. Re-evaluate your divorce plans. There are imaginative solutions.

Divorce Rituals

Divorce is a significant change, not in the sentimental way that characterizes the prior passages, initiations, or departures. It, however, has a beginning, middle, and an end. Perhaps in the legal or the religious domain, we need divorce ceremonies or some mandatory requirement in front of children, parents and friends. The purpose, both psychological and legal, is for both people to affirm that they did the best that they could, they both love their children, and will try to put aside differences in order for everyone to go on with their lives in the best way they can. They hoped that it could have been different, and this is a new beginning.

Cultures historically have numerous ceremonies for rites of passage. All major events have traditions and ceremonies that signify some movement into another stage of life. Christenings, brisses, confirmations, bar and bat mitzvahs, graduations, communions, birthdays, weddings, anniversaries, and even deaths, require relatives, friends, and others to acknowledge that either something is different, better, or symbolic in meaning. Some of these have religious significance, while others are merely celebratory. Others measure time, as in anniversaries, the accomplishment of two people staying together in a legal relationship.

Divorce signifies that these two people did not have the skills, impulse control, or self-knowledge that is necessary to understand the difficult requirements of marriage. They also should admit, like penance, to their own part. And finally, although inconvenient or difficult, loyalty to their children should never be dislodged. It is a promise to one's children that one *must* keep.

Small Doses of Advice

- Mourn the loss of your marriage
- Seek help (friends, groups, religious institutions, counselors)
- Read books (the library is loaded)
- Take care of yourself (exercise, diet, sleep, limit alcohol)
- Bury bitterness and hatred or it will bury you
- Forgive yourself and your partner
- Understand that there will be a cascade of emotions
- Initially make small decisions
- Renew and find friendships
- Be a Quaker and avoid the divorce war
- Don't lie about your spouse
- Have moral courage to control the divorce demons

Children I

- Maintain dignity
- Keep communications open and flexible
- Negotiate co-parenting
- Do not turn children against ex-spouse
- Never use children as hostages against the other (the children pay the ransom)
- Enlist the resources of teachers, grandparents, aunts and uncles.
- Never make promises you can't keep

Children II

- Listen to your children
- Reassure them that you love them and will take care of them
- Be honest
- Prepare them for change
- Encourage the expression of all feelings
- Do not overburden them with your problems
- Use humor. Laughter heals.

CHAPTER 9

Annoyances

I am sure the reader will identify with and come up with similar conclusions and frustrations regarding situations that make one angry. For others less patient, bear with the jeremiad against things that I find infuriating. I do not apologize for my acrimonious tone.

At the magic hour of 6:30 p.m., the phone solicitation begins. At 6:30, a call for Special Olympics, at 6:45 MADD, and around 7, the final few calls, Democratic National Party, concluded by Sprint and a potpourri of other requests. Rage spews at the poor telephone solicitor. Dinner with family is a Herculean feat as someone is generally missing, including myself. And then to be interrupted by some anonymous person requesting money and interfering with my minimal family time is indirect harassment. I resent the abuse of the telephone. My response is to construct strategic defensive maneuvers by employing such devices as caller ID, answering machines, unlisted numbers, — all expensive and time-consuming just to try and extinguish the objectionable behavior of organizations on whose behalf they are calling. I recommend a protection of privacy act. At minimum, a small band of allowable time for charitable or business requests.

Blood Pressure

The second insult in a more generic sense is the poundage purveyors. Television, magazines, and other media outlets are filled with advertisements that both condemn and barrage women about their bodies, weight and wrinkles. Women are generally made to feel inadequate and are presented with every diet and exercise device and a never-ending treadmill of beauty-related endeavors.

Media advertising takes every opportunity to ensure that women are unhappy with something; age, crow lines, puffy eyes, bodies, and breasts. There are very few women who meet the externally imposed standards of beauty, weight, femininity, and perfection. Designer-imposed norms of skeletal, cachectic, pale and wan visions, a masquerade of truth that encourages younger and older women to starve. The skin product promoted that will liberate you from aging and put you in remission from that dreaded disease is constantly advertised.

Women are besieged by an insidious epidemic of weight control maneuvers and fat scrutinization. These unobtainable ideals create distortions and discontent. Women are caught in symbolic self-hatred for the inability to develop the pinnacle of self-control. There is an unending preoccupation with reductionism to the idealized perception of perfection. There is also a resulting correlation with eating disorders in young high-school and college women.

Plastic surgeons encourage women to mutilate, suction off, section off and enlarge on; capitalizing on women's purgatory battles to please themselves or others. This body and beauty involvement, the unbridled self-absorption makes me metamorphosize into a rabid rodent.

Once a good male friend of mine commented "that I looked good: had I lost weight?" In fact, I believe I put on a few extra pounds. This exemplifies the perceived correlation of less equals good. Instead of obsessing on the cycles associated with the weight loss and the concomitant emotional pitfalls, frustrations, self-denigration, it would seem more beneficial to utilize energy for expanding the brain and enhancing intellectual and creative development. The payoff is better, and lasts longer.

Certainly, some form of exercising moderately, combined with healthy eating will contribute to feeling better, but just turn on the TV: 3 aerobics, 1 step, 4 new machines, stop the insanity — diet, power walking, complete with the Greek chorus of forever, thankful women. Even walking gets accolades, as if the invention was recent.

A deceased friend of mine, a concentration camp "guest", (she would have abhorred victim or survivor terminology) briskly walked her dog every day as many Europeans do. Walking energetically has been around since the Paleolithic era. It did not originate in the 20th century. Although marketing gurus contrive every form of machinery, portable and stationary, one-third of Americans are obese. In fact, Americans are getting fatter.

As we get older, generally wisdom, creativity and accomplishment evolve. Lust, sex and bodies are really minor chords in life. Children, friends, traveling and work are where the rewards of life are, presupposing that there are any.

Recently I visited a "home for people who are in their 70's, 80's and 90's." The women, who generally outlasted their husbands, looked robust, somewhat Raphaelean and corpulent, generally healthy. A fermenting idea may be that thin people die sooner.

Indigestion

Many people drive with a propensity for their own extinction. However, they may, without prior agreement, take along others in their risk-taking behavior. We forget that cars are weapons and some of these weapons are owned by terrorist drivers. They far exceed the speed limit, weave a mosaic of unnecessary danger, pass in no-passing zones, play treacherous games, talk incessantly on the phone and exhibit aggressive tactics that are comparable to a Reign of Terror. They are inured to the potential devastation they can cause.

One day I stopped at a red light. Fortunately, I glanced out of the rear view mirror and in utter disbelief I saw a huge truck come barreling towards me. Realizing in that split second that he could never stop, I instinctively pulled over to the side and he proceeded to charge through the red light. In retrospect, if I had not been in a delayed shock, my normal instinct would have been to follow him, shout cascades of driving safety rules, and report his driving to authorities.

In my extremely vigilant role as driver and passenger, I always notice drivers who have a predilection for hostility and aggression, a lethal mixture. They weave back and forth dangerously, tailgating in a manner that epitomizes driving judgment akin to a boxer prior to knockout. Dangerous drivers are killers and we all need protection.

Ulcers

There is a store on 5th Avenue where the make-up salespersons are trained in aggressive assault techniques. They attack with the ferocity and alacrity of deadly pythons, strangling their prey. Sister or sibling stores in the vicinity have also purchased the marine manual. In pondering the purpose of the Venus Flytrap Approach, the deduced reason is to capture the weak, infirmed, impressionable victim. Prior to the kill, the offensive is camouflaged by a manipulative compliment in a form like "Oh, your earrings are beautiful." I and others have mastered the counteroffensive of retreat, extreme vigilance and perseverance in avoiding the militia.

Whatever happened to polite, deferential, respectful and relaxed treatment of customers? To the guilty parties, *Cease Fire!*

Headaches

Shopping, the espoused Olympic-species sport is seen as an accomplishment of, alternately, shrewdness and indulgence. One might deduce that skills required for this triathlon demand at least post-graduate study of advanced athletic training for America's Cup. Shoppers possess the disease of unalterable accumulation. However, my dissenting view is that shopping as an activity operates to demean women. The subtle implication is that, for women, gratification and optimal fulfillment means that spending money and achievement (or status) are validated through acquisition, a slight derivative of indulgent narcissist. While women's inclinations to extravagance are open to subtle scrutiny, men's purchases are imbued and hallowed as necessary or deserved.

The concept of woman as designated spender, has led to the belief that shopping is associated with indulgence, impulsivity and a way to soothe harassed emotions: a therapeutic transplant. The seekers and searchers who have honed the approaches to bank depletion, are of only one gender.

In meeting the challenges of life's episodes, men are very accomplished in the endeavors of shopping, although it has a different label. Somehow there is a higher purpose in the male orientation of purchasing cars, trucks, computers, snowblowers; the vital necessities of reels, rods, guns, the sports-objects entitlements. Catalogues, the mail route to consumption, satisfy male appetites; they do not even have to be seen in public, yet the outcome is identical. There are other ways the male species' purchases are sanctioned. All the hi-fidelity equipment can be shared by the entire family, even if it means economic collapse.

Men have just as many shopping privileges as women, but the latter are branded as part of their identity, the trenches of achievement. Anyway, do males or females have more Ferraris?

For most women I know, except for a few imbued with wealth or excess time, shopping is a side event, an activity interweaved around work, family obligations, exercise and all the other calls of duty required.

CHAPTER 10

Psychologists and other Mental Health Providers

Psychoanalysis —*I was depressed . . . I was suicidal, as a matter of fact, I would have killed myself but I was in analysis with a strict Freudian and if you kill yourself they make you pay for the sessions you miss.*

Woody Allen (b.1935), U.S. film-maker: Alvy Singer (Allen), in Annie Hall (film; screenplay by Woody Allen and Marshall Brickman, directed by Woody Allen, 1977). The gag originated in a stand-up routine recorded live in San Francisco, Aug. 1968, on the album The Nightclub Years (1968), 'Second Marriage'

The inclusion of this chapter has been motivated by several concerns that have ethical relevancy to the fluid field of psychology and its questionable tributaries. It is intended for the public to scrutinize treatments for psychological disorders that are promoted with asphyxiating intoxication.

Mutant growths of psychology have been replete with unverifiable fads: primal scream, EST, healing the inner child, 1-2 steps poly-disorder treatment for everything, followed by expressing your anger, your needs and your shame. All assume to alleviate some suffering, to increase self-esteem, or to promote healing and integration, culminating with spirituality. A plethora of movements continually emerge with some unsubstantiated suppositions, imprecise treatments and reductionistic cures. Each psychologist relies on a particular framework and is glued to its phrases. The vision of their patients are based on a rigid orientation. Some are focused on "shame;" every observation, every suffering is shame based. Others are concerned with "toxicity," — parental, friends and society — all have their PCP's that have debiliated their patients. Other rhetorical influences in treatment include the entire gamut of victimization, spirituality and the overuse of "self-esteem." It is the simplicity and faddishness that is objectionable. Each may be important as a partial explanation or choice of treatment modality, but not the entire reason for all the dimensions required for understanding each person.

This is the age of co-dependents, of multi-addicted dysfunctional families, wounded individuals, and toxic parents. There is a proliferation of 12-step programs; the universal dance for unimaginable symptoms and disorder beyond our control. These dually self-diagnosed, multi-addicted, co-dependent people rummaging around, locating their lost child are the most recent rhetoric of our mental-health proselytizers.

Every conceivable act — eating chocolate, exercising, bibliotic endeavors, puttering around the house, shopping, working and gardening — requires a discrete diagnostic category. A multiplying self-help Library of Congress exists for any psychological affliction, replete with exposited remedies that have dubious intellectual integrity, an impoverished vocabulary and minimal objective validation. Several are fad treatments that do not conform to general standards of inquiry.

In one day, in casual overheard conversation, two to three people stated that they are co-dependent, are from dysfunctional families and are working on their self-esteem issues. This created jargon and limited labeling techniques seems to be counterintuitive. Similarly, I've wondered, is Dakota south or north? Now there are support groups for coffee-addicted people.

Dysfunctional families are the infectious disease of the 90's and no one is immune. As the psychological jargon multiplies and treatment modalities arise, some of them are fairly pseudoscientific. The terms "co-dependents" and "enablers" suggest a conspiratorial blame that you are part of another person's disease or at least maintaining it. With all these new viral maladies we present the shrinks of the season, who capitalize on your disease and preach with pseudo-intellectual, unsophisticated, and speculative concepts that they present as facts.

Essentially, there has been minimal or questionable research that scrutinizes the efficacy of these treatments. In addition, proselytizing that 98-99 percent of families are dysfunctional, implies that everyone needs help or is in denial. Dysfunction, the referent 90's slogan, suggests that everyone is recovering from some disorder developed in families and as a result, we are either victims, addicted, co-dependent, or guilty by association. Finally, there is the diagnosis of "borderline," which is one of the most pejorative labels. Shame is the basis of all addictions and we are both addicted to feeling and addicted to not-feeling; it does sound somewhat contradictory.

Recently, one of the dependency gurus stated on TV conclusively stated that the workaholics' addiction was far more destructive to families than in those families where members' drug of choice was alcohol. At least to my limited knowledge, there hasn't been any long-term studies that adequately verify this conclusion. This epigrammatic pronouncement is another exploitive sermon with dubious scientific verification.

Punctuating this concern about inferential errors, in my experience, a mere twenty years of treating women whose fathers were alcoholic, these patients accumulated characteristics and problems that range from chronic and disabling to moderately adaptable. Depression, over-responsibility, issues with men, conflicts over conflict, emphasis on control, and stress-related illness are but a few of the "gifts" of alcoholism. Family life is unpredictable, unsafe, and generally, emotionally impoverished. The adults act out or withdraw, creating a sense of impending doom or chaotic disruption. These portraits of family life are barren and crazy, like a Daliesque black and white burden of shame and secrecy, with blotches of bright red.

However, in families of workaholics, there can be predictability and stability. The person generally works, then comes home late. The secondary gain is that many of these families have nice houses and the accoutrements of people who work hard. Children are not constantly humiliated and do not feel responsible for taking care of their parents. Before any public educator makes a statement of such magnitude — that alcoholism is "better" than workaholism — we need some statistical analysis or long-term studies to verify another flagrantly sensationalistic statement.

Some of the providers of these sprouting new theories have training, but it does not necessarily meet any high standard of competence. Although they may be well-intentioned, or even morally motivated, at times, there is some hint of exploitiveness, or promises of some optimal change. Several of these psychological EVENTS present a high degree of collective catharsis, expressive sexuality, brief intense demand for immediate trust and intimacy and a permission for regression. This is what I call the "sundial" approach; turning to EST, primal scream or a 12-step program for any activity of life. The post-EST graduate, spotted in a millisecond by his or her programmed language and rhetoric, is an individual lukewarmly brainwashed. It proves that people can be persuaded to do anything and pay for it.

Public performing therapists range from the most eloquent by their personal charismatic and persuasiveness to others who should disqualify themselves in the intellectual arena. There are the self-revelatory, confessional, preacher-like entertainers whose rhetoric is modeled after a religious exorcism experience. Then, there are those who revert to simple "cook-book solutions," offering vague verbal ingredients for effective change.

Many psychologists offer simple solutions to the problems that have not been empirically examined. Certain postulations have been transformed into truths, such as: expressing your anger is good; intimacy is the sine qua non of a healthy relationship; be vulnerable, ask for what you need; be assertive, tell your spouse how you feel; and all relationships require certain skills (Buy my tapes, that is).

Intimacy, another elusive concept, is in the lexicon of idealized outcomes for couples, and certainly prevalent in the fix-it books on relationships. It is espoused as the most powerful dimension of coupling. Although it has been legitimized as a precondition or embodiment of satisfaction, there are certain assumptions and value-laden generalizations that need some cross-examination.

Individuals have different levels, styles, cycles and expression of intimacy needs. The therapist may have one concept of acceptability and criteria. The same level, approach, or measurement may not be appropriate for all couples and especially, individuals. A friend of mine related that her therapist intimated that until a certain level of intimacy with her spouse was reached, therapy was not completed. This was after years of couples and individual treatment and the expenditure of $22,000.

Another theoretical ironic phenomenon I have observed is a subtype of therapists who present a coherent cluster of separation anxiety symptomology. This acute malaise manifests itself in the frequency with which they call their answering service, their attachment to their beepers and the terrible state of many of their patients. In addition, they display extreme discomfort when going on vacations, and wherever their faraway destinations take them — East Africa, Mongolia, Hong Kong — they will persevere in calling their patients. How can they (the patients) function without their presence? Will they kill themselves, be hospitalized, decompensate, make poor decisions or transfer to another therapist? This may be rooted in a pervasive omnipotent superiority syndrome where the therapist amasses a coterie of dependent patients and friends.

This is a therapeutic paradox, possibly rooted in primitive narcissism; the unconscious need of the therapist for dependency by others. Everyone around them sees how wonderful and caring they are. Inherent in this is the perceived notion that clients are unable to function without them. I cringe when someone says to me: "My therapist says this, and I should do that." That's not what therapy is about. In my view, therapy exists to challenge people to become more adept at making their own decisions, imperfect as they may be. Generating self-efficacious behavior — autonomy — is an ultimate goal. A less astute observer might make a logical deduction that one of the purposes of therapy is to enable people to function well, at least for some limited time. There is some self-deception when we decide that these patients are borderline and thus need you to be a constant in their lives. This is at best a condescending attitude toward people you are helping. Yes, in a few cases, dependency on the therapist may be the best intervention program.

Therapeutic sensibility implies that there is a need for consistency, compassion, predictability, and trust in the relationship. However, the mental health professional also demonstrates health by a fully developed life, rather than by excessive feelings of self-worth and aggrandizement realized through patients desperately needing them or following their prescriptions to the letter.

TV Psychologists

Popular TV psychologists may do a disservice to the public by giving advice based on limited data. Seduced by the audience and possibly their own need to be all-knowing and have immediate answers, they proffer simplistic analysis and solutions. In addition, axioms offered may be blatantly inadequate. After continually interrupting, provoking anger, and paying little attention to the speaker, the self-serving therapist, viewed on television, advises the spouse to "Tell him what you need." Couples continually tell, explain, cajole, yell, imply indirectly and also concretely, what they want from each other.

There is minimal accountability, responsibility or long-term feedback, and exacerbating the possible ethical issues, is that many of the talk shows are created to titillate the audience and ratings are based on sensationalistic imprinting. Their public service purpose may be negligible. Would physicians offer a quick diagnosis, propose a treatment or prescribe medication without at least a cursory review of a patient's history and symptoms? Yet, the media "quick fix" constitutes superficial advice or solutions to complex problems that erode credibility and professionalism. There are some ethical issues to be examined.

Physicians, and hopefully other professional contemporaries, would ethically eschew a telephone diagnosis, and never offer a treatment plan or prescribe necessary medication, without a thorough review of systems and prior medical and psychological history. It is the psychologist's need to be famous and influence others with their own performance. A reader might have a response that envy or jealousy is a motivation for my criticism.

Prior to my own television debut performance, the host's instructions were for me to be argumentative and controversial, probably I surmised, to increase the show's ratings. As I morally and personally reject this non-professional behavior, I did not acquiesce.

Ethical psychologists do not, whether a person was murdered or died from natural causes, break patient confidentiality. Many patients share their secrets with others but that does not give any psychologist permission to divulge this confidential information via the media. What is revealed in a session is protected material and never belongs to the public unless a written verified disclosure form is signed by the patient prior to his/her death. Personally, I would want my secrets cremated and scattered far enough away; Antarctica at the least.

The following is a short anecdote of my own experience in treatment for a post-traumatic stress disorder. On the first day of December, 1980, within 15 minutes, a light rain turned into diamond crystals of ice, and the temperature plummeted. Unknowingly, abstractly unconcerned about the treachery beneath my Toyota Land Cruiser, an army-like truck, I innocently downshifted or maybe lightly braked. This huge vestige of a tank, without warning, traversed into and through a telephone pole, with a blade-like paper mill motion and was halted by a concrete wall.

In a departure from my usual rigid precautionary style, I was unseatbelted. This flamboyant, Olympic entry resulted in 50-vertical-designed stitches across my head (the big V Dracula, as poignantly described by my daughter), several broken ribs and some minor knee-sewing repair work. A post-accident diagnosis, not very astute, made by the patient (me), revealed a cluster of psychiatric symptoms that included generalized fear of snow, ice in any form, panic at a mere television forecast of inclement weather, addiction to weather reports between November and

March, and dreams of microscopic flakes. These previous forms of beauty caused my bowels to tighten up, palms to sweat, daymares, and perseverating ruminations.

At this time, I was employed as a behavioral scientist at a hospital and my professional responsibilities necessitated arriving at work. Thus I sought in the prevailing psychological nomenclature, "professional help," highly recommended by an associate.

The therapist's orientation, training and personal agenda was psychoanalytic psychotherapy. Although she assured me my fears were normal considering I had almost died, her focus was my childhood, parental relationships and present conflicts, of which there were many.

After a year of early childhood recollections, we decided that this was not going anywhere, at least not where she expected it to go. Either I was an uncooperative patient, or counter-dependent, or too goal-oriented. In fact, I really was not interested in examining these issues at that juncture.

The solution, as usual in my own way, was not go to work on treacherous days, reschedule my patients who canceled their appointments anyway (they were smart), and buy a good four-wheel drive vehicle. Yes, I still suffer from ICPD (icy conditions, panic disorder), but have figured a way to live with it, or slide around it.

If the aforementioned remarks seem critical, clearly I have witnessed the psychological devastation of alcoholism, child abuse, rape, or many of the struggles other individuals have, which are associated with trauma. I can attest to the impressive help that some people have received from well-trained clinicians whose education was supplemented with complex intellectual inquisitions, kindness, and whose intimacy and other needs are met outside the office. Good teachers, good physicians and good psychologists do not consistently appear in the media. They are too busy attending to their patients, keeping abreast of the literature, attending conferences and taking care of their own families.

CHAPTER 11

Short Subjects

I have always admired, with an incredulous regard, some writers' ability to capture observations with potent, yet minimal words. Others, who overload their writing, frustrate and bore the reader. A good writer can cut narrative off at just the right juncture.

The next few essays are designed to liberate the reader, employing words and paragraphs judiciously. These brief pages are prefatory highlights, like a casual introduction to someone you believe you've known or would like to in the future.

Memories

We all chronicle our pasts by selecting what, and to what intensity, we remember certain events. Access to denied incidents and their specific contents varies in relation to one's perception of the valence of painful and pleasant meanings. Our memories are far from precise mathematical formulas. The unconscious spaces in our minds are continually rearranged and in a puzzling way, distorted.

There are quotidian mental choices that occupy our thoughts caused by agitating over the past in a manner that masquerades itself as truth. We discontinue or continue attaching blame to the significant others in our past, usually our parents. Even in a close-to-the-ideal family, most parents cannot supply everything we believe we should have received in our formative years. There is always the tendency to idealize adults, and when we recognize their weaknesses and inadequacies, these lapses are highlighted with sardonic potency.

Because our memories of past events are highly malleable and emotionally dismantling, self-deception occurs. The truth is always elusive and often speculative. There are no written testaments or daily logs that reflect all the transactional tributaries. A particular example, often seen with couples describing an event or an interplay between them, verifies that reality is a personal formulation.

Each person outdistances the other by comments such as: "That's not how it happened."; "I didn't say that."; and "That's not what you did." They never agree on the sequence or the picture. It's as if there were a sideshow that maintained their attention. The main event, the one actually transpiring between them, is never perceived congruently. They catalogue with precision and passion the events that occurred. Certainty and conviction are categorically displayed. These interdependent transactions have not occurred in the tarnished memories of the past, but are yesterday's or last week's actions. Each player is blocked by his or her own obtrusive genealogy, causing each one to modify recollections, thus polarizing reactions to the same event. Truth is as blind as a quick papillary reaction.

Another significant example pointing to the evidence toward muddled memory is exemplified when siblings in a family discredit each other's accounts of family dramas. Events are seen and remembered very differently according to the age when they occurred, the position and role in one's family, and each individual's temperamental makeup. Memories are affect-laden in that the ones of high emotional content are more accessible.

Thus, the predictable events, the less inflamed, are rolled over in the fog. The vivid picture we have of our childhood, our pasts, have an exclusive interpretation, and I recommend that we are more critical of our own appraisals.

Adulthood

Very few children arrive at adulthood without perceptions of unfulfillment, vague or pervasive. Unmet needs are the parable sin characterizing all children's emergence into the society of what we euphemistically label as adults. Parents who work hard may leave the child with a belief that they were not important. Oversolitious, indulgent parents, whose children's every demand is attended to materially and emotionally, do not teach delayed gratification and tolerance for frustration. Overly ambitious parents, or a family with clearly designated goals, may create within one the abysmal sense that nothing they accomplished is enough. In my own psychological parlance, it is the "Serious Striving Syndrome" with parental approval as motivator.

Families, in their uncogent ability, tend to favor one child, overlook others, and descriptively label all their progeny. Parents are imperfect, each with their own history, benign for some, while miserable for others.

The lineaments of the adult persona are influenced by a particular genetic input, siblings, peers, school, community, mini- and macro-events, and luck. With my dissenting opinion, the cause-effect thinking model of parenting, — input-outcome — should be put on probation. Societal influences can infiltrate good parenting. Children ingest a factory outlet of inherently malignant risks.

Some children have an amazing internal resilience while others have more fragile dispositions. There is the inference that if everyone were parented better and received consistent affirming emotional responses, the outcome would be healthier and less psychologically infected adults. This deductive thinking, it seems, causes guilt, fear and parenting paralysis in every aspect of child-rearing. There are many people who assume that the female is not mothering well enough and cannot attend to all her children's needs and functions. If their children are having difficulty, it is implicitly her fault.

Some have been educated to believe that their intense involvement is "better parenting" and that all children's behavior problems originate in defective parenting, typically identifying the primary offender as "mothers." However, most problems are not serious and have to do with the wide variety of personality traits inherited, innate temperament, in addition to the stresses of the particular situation the child is in. It's "nouveau pseudo psychological cuisine." When children are not overindulged or overrated, they learn how to take care of themselves, tolerate disappointment, expand their potential creativity, and become responsible and independent. Delayed gratification is an adult necessity, — rewards for working hard on what you want to achieve.

All childhoods of difficulty (alias dysfunction,) whether borne out of poverty, neglect, conflict, or tragedy do not necessarily result in adulthoods of a similar caliber. These early experiences may actually cultivate kindness and compassion in the child. Some adults who suffered tremendous deprivation as children are uniquely gifted and accomplished. There are many who have had epic journeys from squalor with early lives littered with feelings of abandonment and parental betrayal, and yet achieve good lives that reverberate around them.

Many men I've talked with in a social context, and otherwise, describe strict parents by whom they were severely disciplined. They have been successful, have a breadth of emotional expressiveness and show kindness and warmth to their wives. They themselves are concerned parents. Parenting styles of punitiveness and harshness would theoretically cause all kinds of debilitating problems, according to the experts. Sometimes, deprivation or adversity engenders independence, self-direction, creative expression, and the capacity to transform one's own suffering into a life of goodness, altruism, success, and productivity.

Loneliness

One of the conditions that people suffer from, not described accurately in any diagnostic code, is loneliness. It is an existence of acute alienation and a sense of gnawing emptiness, characterized by daily interactions that are devoid of any substantial meaning. This connectedness deprivation — a pervasive malaise — causes people to take expeditions on a continuum of psychic slavery. Compulsive television watching, desperate calls to converse with anyone and computer affection are ways one tries to quell this unsettling dimension. In its more virulent form, the outcome may be compulsive alcohol and drug use, medical problems, violence, and suicide.

Social scientists have numerous explanations for a documented recent increase in alienation and loneliness. Divorce, with its losses and disruptions, is one of the factors that contribute to a sense of not belonging. Family dislocations and disconnectedness, the highly disjointed lives many people now lead and even the contemporary pressure for focus on the self can cause this subtle anxious feeling.

Relationships for lonely people may be mundane and devoid of emotional satisfaction. There is an emphasis today on pseudo-intimacy, the ethics of openness and the cliché "Thank you for sharing," that result in the "instant-potatoes" relationships. As part of groups, some therapeutic in nature, individuals find that closeness and intimacy are expected by self-revelation. Many people search for groups that will assuage loneliness. These moments of opening-up and "sharing" are still on the periphery of solid and consistent relationships.

In many ways, therapists soothe the pain of loneliness and may be the person's only significant connection. Therapy, however, is not a substitute for social bonds outside of this paid friendship. What transpires in that perfect room should be a conduit to actions and personal change that increase one's ability to experience loving and satisfying encounters. Loneliness occurs because we may not have a consistent network of friends or a sense of family attachment. Social changes result in a gradual migration into anonymity.

If work takes precedence over competing parts of our lives, it is not unusual to experience striking alienation at times between the "exciting demands" of our work. The exigencies of mobile business, multiple marriages and estranged families, aggravate the condition of isolation. People grapple with the choices that either fragment their lives or carefully design it. Loneliness is a by-product of poorly thought out construction.

Although a radical thought in the era of dysfunction, families are a protection against the despair of isolation. They give guidance, attention and have a powerful biological responsibility to care. The backlash by experts against families, labeling them as toxic, is attention-seeking bombardment. Television garbage is more lethal.

As a result of serious unanticipated events, loneliness checks in. The death of a spouse, sibling or close friend produces a dislocation of nurturance. Illness and hospitalization are additional series of divisions from normal life. Patients make reference to being deserted and invisible.

There are no simple formulas to quickly defrost the icy conditions of life: the habitual distractions cover the pain in each of us. No one can tell you how to find the best antidote to a particular dilemma. Losses will always be part of living; relationships will never be restored, physical capacities will be diminished, and rejection and death are the master classes in life. Perhaps the only advice is to learn from the loneliness instead of habitually searching for the temporary elixir.

Under the Surface

On a visible level, people act in a way that may be in opposition to their underlying feelings or tendencies. Interior dimensions exist in everyone and these gnawing companions have the ability to masterfully imprison. There are parts and places in ourselves that are kept warily guarded, and are only open to a few outsiders, if ever.

On the surface, a mirror calm might be visible or a peaking agitation firmly develops. In order to quell the conflicted mind, camouflage is necessary. For some, the disguises are crippling, a constant adversarial plaintiff that reflects the undertow of secret thoughts, feelings, and potential distressing acts. There is a division between what appears and the hidden plankton, — a split-screen effect.

This duality of overt snapshots reveals only part of our story. Those covert basins can dominate or interfere in the lives of many who we do not even suspect. Those in enviable positions, powerful or celebrated, have undercurrents of displaced fear, anger and pervasive hurts. As they are more open to criticism and evaluation, the descent into failure is dominant in their psyches.

When men or women demand attention and operate as if they must be the nucleus of the surrounding network, discomfort and doubt occur because they are always in competition with others who might supplant them. This being the case, continual striving for achievement and importance may cause people to act in a manner that borders on immoral, cruel or overwhelmingly self-absorbed.

Behaviors will emerge that expose the layered life. It appears like some mutant actions. When individuals degrade, demean or exploit others, this behavior originates from a place inside with defective circulation. Lying is another indicator that one has capitulated to the little demons. Is the deception to impress, cover up bad intentions, to place oneself in a brighter light or even to destroy another? So many people feel as though they are counterfeit and mimic a different persona; another's geography so to speak.

Sometimes we falsely observe that certain of our friends or associates appear content or at least only minimally miserable. Without looking carefully, we decide that they have assumed the reputation of honorable, consistent and "well-adjusted." Then, unexpected and incredible events occur. They leave their spouses, quit jobs, and symbolically climb Mt. Everest by sleeping with the 15-year-old baby-sitter. Their fallibility has a disquieting reverberation. Many unexpected acts are actually outcomes of the battlefields in our minds, the arguments that for years we endure, and then something suddenly takes a machete to them, and wins.

Unfortunately, I am more concerned about the events than have the ability to offer blithe solutions. I can only speculate on the apparent causes that stimulate the flights of people, the human errors that reject and dodge conscience and arbitrarily damage others. From a psychologist's viewpoint, the impact of moral incompetence or moral myopia is a slow, progressive disease that is very precarious for our children. We have become clever at circumventing moral self-controversy and there are many salespeople that sanction this conduct.

I believe a moral sense, albeit difficult, can be found. The sources for my optimism are specifically linked to the evidence of my experience.

Replenishing the Therapist

One is frequently queried as to the ways one copes with intense sadness of recurrent exposure to pained lives, and the dismantling tragedies that compel people to seek a listener. "Don't you ever get depressed?" is the perennial question I'm asked.

The response, undisguised, is generally no. Listening to people has an impact in itself that is more enhancing than debilitating. There are many things in life that are meaningless, devoid of any rejuvenating features. In some ways, the unraveling and speculations, patients tell me about their personal autobiographies, is a creative, challenging assignment.

Fortunately, I inherited a gift — a salacious DNA and a biochemical high serotonin load — the genetic explanatory shield against major depressive episodes or dysthymic disorder. That is not to say that there is not an undertow of episodic sadness for me, crying spells from the cumulative effect of the days. Separating from others' emotional devastation does not mean one does not care or have compassion. It does not help to be reactive and agglutinated. Therapists need to have a personal life in order to replenish themselves.

Traveling, moderate exercise, reading, cooking, cultural and non-cultural activities with friends and my children as well as brief psychotic periods of cleaning relieve the pangs. A very cathartic endeavor is organizing, discarding, giving clothes and items to church groups or charities, — the "uncluttering," — and a good laugh or bizarre humor helps. However, the most personality palliative response for me is solitude, a required respite from obligations and the predicable prevailing winds.

The suggestions for others is to cultivate attention to meaningful acts or times of quiet thinking. Underlying optimal experiences may lie in their simplicity, and not achievement oriented pursuits. Each person can retrieve their own blueprint that satisfies a better and newer sense of themselves.

Physician Praise

At the writing of this book I am in my 14th year as a Behavioral Scientist in a Residency Program for Family Physicians. If this writing expedition continues at this rate, reaching my 25th year will be a certainty.

There will always be a prismatic view of health care, depending upon the side you are promoting. The changes in the delivery of health care can be interpreted by its employees, the insurance companies, the government, the integrated health systems, the patients, and finally, by the physicians. The impact of all these external influences ranges from the benign to acute renal failure. In the last decade, the powerful insurance companies, HMO's and an escalation of malpractice incidents have disillusioned many practitioners and made their jobs more complicated and decision-making more restrictive.

I am compelled not only to affix praise but to explicitly correct some perceptions that devalue the profession of physician. As a psychologist in the arena of medical care, yet an outsider in the daily fights, the pressures, the medical dramas, and the ever-present ethical dilemmas, the visual field for me is unencumbered by competing forces.

The view that physicians make a lot of money is clouded by financial facts. For some the debt from medical school ranges from $50,000 to $100,000. Residency has been christened "slave labor." When residents graduate and enter practice, beside the weight of bills (medical school and/or purchasing a practice), managing and paying a staff, overhead, exorbitant malpractice insurance, and seeing their children and spouses in flight stopovers, they are bombarded with regulations and hospital political dramas. We underestimate the monsoon of relentless crises they face.

I am often struck by the difficulties in the entire spectrum of the physicians' career — the long hours and the constant barrage of challenges to surmount. They are required to see more patients per hour, attempt to obtain prior approval for other procedures, which may be needed in certain decisions, and assume various additional forms of responsibility.

Very few of us are required to make decisions and use training or expertise that may at some times result in a person's death or prevent one. Yes, physicians make mistakes, probably far less than careless drivers, yet they have to live with each error and the anguish it brings and try to manage the self-doubt and sleepless nights that ensue.

Many physicians' training includes the moral and ethical dilemmas that they will be faced with, the quality of their care that is being continually assessed, and their constant vigilance to do what is best for their patients. When we talk about exorbitant salaries, who are we kidding? Compared with movie stars, football players, Wall Street traders, corporate leaders, middle management, real-estate investors, lawyers, architects, and now employees of insurance companies, many physicians may actually be underpaid. Many of these other professions are not tied to beepers, not plagued with malpractice and litigations, are able to go out for lunch and dinner on expense accounts, and even get stock options.

Even if their company, like General Motors, does poorly, the CEO's get significant remuneration or sit on boards of other companies for further compensation. The physicians do not get the same perks, like the use of company planes, valuable gifts, fully paid meetings and vacations, and limousine service, nor do they invest $1,000 and come out with $100,000 like some of our arrogant leaders who speculate on the commodites market and attribute it to good luck.

Good physicians not only possess a broad-based knowledge acquired over many intense years of training but have an intuitive sense of their patients' needs, personality, and fears. Restrictive regulations, rigid economic barriers, government infringement in their decision-making freedom will not make good medical care. In my 14 years of collaborating with physicians, most of them have intense dedication to healing and inquisitive minds concerning tshe nature of disease and health. We need to enhance the trust and confidence we have in them and encourage them to be more self-monitoring and to stand by their well-established code of ethics. The remedies do not reside in the government, lawyers, or insurance companies, who, in fact, have become the "money making industry."

I am not arguing the point that some cost control is a necessary requirement. The concern I have is about the effect these changes have on the underpinning of the medical encounter, the relationship that doctors and patients need to have, which exists in the best medical care. In so many cases, providers are changed according to the insurance plans the patient has and long-term knowledge of who you are, your family and all the other forces that affect your health, is eroded.

What is screened out by the public is the regular incidence of patients who are demanding, rude, hostile, or who define their own illness and have their own agendas that are not medically recommended. Disability is the only accepted treatment. Others are always armed in a lawsuit attire, a pin-striped gray refugee. Patients have even come into the office drunk, denying any alcohol consumption, inebriated, or with a gun. They feel they are entitled to come in late, miss appointments, demand narcotics, lose their prescriptions, and complain to everyone. Because there are contractual agreements between patients and physicians, the physicians are in an opposite situation — they are overworked, underpaid, never take sabbaticals, do not generally get stock options, and work over their lunch hours, frequently leaving the office predictably late.

The standard of excellent medical care resides primarily in the physicians who can follow their patients and coordinate a comprehensive approach to illness and wellness. Most are ethically motivated, compassionate, intellectually inquisitive and work more hours than those in other professions.

Small Doses of Advice for Loneliness
- Loneliness is very common
- Understand yourself: Focus on your good qualities
- Take active steps
- Consider volunteering, organizations that need help
- Participate in groups that have mutual interest
- Avoid self-pity, whining and passivity
- Change occupation, job or where you live
- Be friendlier and take small risks
- Seek guidance or counseling
- Care about others

CHAPTER 12

Autobiographical Data

✤

Revisiting one's past for too long a stay, and emersing one-self in early historical data can be an ascendancy into private indulgence. This brief, selective retracing has only occurred as it might explain the germination of my ideas.

I do not think that I could have written this book until I was in my 50's. It required a sense of order, the comfort of re-flection, and the passing of the internal commotion of earlier ages.

This brief autobiographical section is included less out of vanity and more as an explanation of the roots of some of my ideas. I have intentionally deleted huge portions of this personal history, as with time there have been some major morality shifts and minor chords to be discarded as they only have a flickering illuminating purpose.

In everyone's renovated autobiography, inferential errors occur. Our brains have mechanisms to annotate experiences and retrieve them selectively. The reality of the accuracy of one's memory is an individual's best guess estimate of the past.

I was very hesitant to discuss the writing of this book and to encapsulate a summary of my observations, experiences and inferential philosophy. It cannot be articulated in four or five simple sentences. While writing this book, I had two jobs, two children, three houses, one farm, and one husband, so it was written in small frames of time on several forms of transportation: planes, trains, buses, as a passenger in a car or truck, on ferries and catamarans. I avoided hot air balloons, helicopters and submarines (over and underwater methods).

As a true insomniac, (and proud of it), note-taking and random scribbling occurred at hours when others are enjoying their REM sleep. In small enough doses, my particular sleep disorder has proven to be uniquely beneficial.

This endeavor has required inordinate time, discipline and the circumnavigation of daily responsibilities to find the required solitude. In the first year of writing this book, I enlisted assistance from no one. Neither my husband, other family members nor my closest friend were aware of the countless hours I spent conceptualizing and clarifying, planning and polishing the manuscript.

The source of this behavior is extreme independence, not a derivative of arrogance, or the belief that others do not have superior or at least complementary abilities. Certainly in editorial skills and writing acumen, my academic training was spurious, at best. Others, I am sure, could have refined my awkward style and deleted the deficiencies. As a self-diagnosed counter-dependent personality, I am not accustomed to asking for assistance. Exacerbating this long-standing idiosyncratic personality style is the fact that, with age, I find that self-absorption decreases and inquiries about my book in progress would bring unwanted attention.

In the expedition from childhood to adulthood, some events imprint on us potently and others are embedded in the gauze of our memory storage. We all chronicle our past by selecting what we remember and the intensity to which we recall certain events.

We deny access to parts and contents of our experiences both painful and pleasant. Our memories are far from precise mathematical formulas. Thus, distortions and skewedness occur. The shorelines of memories are illusions pushing some things in and others out.

Although not necessarily receiving all the preconditions that are sufficient for childhood and adolescence resiliency nor salubriousness, I have been able to overcome many of the obstacles I encountered in that time duration. Introspectively, the underlying condition at each juncture is attributable to an abundance of serotonin, an unconventional adaptive psyche, an inherited cognitive capacity for rationale thought (although my husband would take issue with some of these confessions) overlaid by a determined spirit.

Long-term memory for most of the first 10 years is fallible; it was destroyed by an amnesia bomb, retrograde or anterograde type, but I forgot which one. Events in that time frame did foreshadow sources for relentless independence. Whatever occurred in my development, it yielded an urge for self-reliance — the need to accomplish everything "myself."

I have been minimally plagued by any sense of personal inadequacy or depression. It is as if I had a pre-programmed DNA molecule with strength and clarity (subjective). This does not preclude brief visiting demons, conflicts, bias, resentments, or the making of serious mistakes.

Generally in one's life there is either a mentor, a benevolent, or a guiding parent or relative — someone in a formative phase that affirms your unique worth or particular strength. As I peruse my somewhat repressed past, no one emerges.

In my lifetime thus far, I have traversed the whole economic range from poverty to middle class to what one might consider wealth. I have participated in all forms and levels of cultures from teaching military officers' children on Governor's Island in New York City to working in Head Start. I have had another identity in the corporate elite as the spouse of a Johnson and Johnson executive, a college teacher, psychologist in private practice, and a faculty member (Behavioral Scientist) in a Residency Program for Family Physicians.

The accumulation of diverse experiences afforded me a real, non-theoretical, world view about poverty and wealth. Additional derivatives from this evolutionary process were freedom and access to a very different world from my early childhood. I acquired a license to move from a project in Brooklyn, supplanted by a dismal apartment in Queens, to owning a house and farm in Bucks County, Pennsylvania, two houses in Nantucket, Massachusetts, and the typical accouterments of the so-called monied class.

The common denominator of these evolutions for both my husband and myself has been largely attributable to steady, hard work. For me, it was a disciplined drive to set goals and accomplish these within my capabilities. It meant years of summer school, evenings studying and delayed gratification.

One of my earliest recollections was living with my grandmother, in a room with a half caved-in-ceiling, and roaches joining me in bed, so that I awakened to swelled bites all over my body. This was euphemistically called a Brooklyn tenement. We upgraded our living conditions to a housing project in a section called Williamsburg. This was an integrated community where the minority was very blond, Caucasian children. My heritage was Jewish Eastern European. However, at that time it was a very safe neighborhood. Even after dark, I could be found roller skating, which resulted in major damage to my body, and because of continual falls on the concrete sidewalks, bloody knees, leaving scars after the wounds healed.

The Brooklyn experience was followed by a move to Queens, another "project," another apartment. Due to conflict with my mother and other problems, I was not given the opportunity to go to college with my parents' financial support. I attribute her inability to give of certain things a result of growing up in the Depression, an experience that caused frustrations and, in hollow psychological jargon, unresolved conflicts.

Working full-time, attending school in the evenings, completing Bachelor's and Master's degrees, were accomplished as a result of my own fierce determination. Soon after college, I married a man who proposed after a brief courtship of less than three months. Not knowing either myself well, or another, which is an unattainable task anyway, resulted in many challenges.

Under much duress, after three years and two burglaries, my husband and I left New York City and established a long term residency in New Hope, Pennsylvania. Although offered a more prestigious job, I chose to work at a Head Start Program. My husband began his career at Johnson and Johnson, so part of my life, probably a small percentage, was connected to the corporate world. His claim to fame was being the President of McNeill Consumer Products, though for only a few weeks, when the Tylenol crisis occurred.

Synthesizing the following ten years into a minuscule capsule, without the cyanide interference, I commuted two evenings a week to New York City. I also attended Saturday classes, years of summer school to fulfill all the Ph.D. requirements, held a teaching job, had a young child (my daughter Meira), and the demands of a marriage, work and the cultivation of friendships, seem in retrospect, a Herculean endeavor. Naturally, as a semi-prototype of Type A behavior, despite inclement weather, a two-hour drive, snow, and ice, I never missed a class.

Eight years prior to my faculty position in the family practice residency program, a semi-tragic event occurred in my life, which verifies the impact that certain memories and events have on one's psyche. More than twenty years later, although emotionally dulled, I can virtually remember and transpose every detail of that evening.

In May of 1972, I was seven months pregnant. In the early part of this pregnancy, there had been bleeding, problematic pain, and a prescription for some bed rest. During that time, my medical care was less than adequate. In one prenatal visit, I commented that I was sure I felt two heads. There was a significant history of twins in my family, my great grandmother having two sets. I believe that the doctor filed this fact under medically unknowledgeable, hysterical pregnant women and dismissed my concern.

One evening, in excruciating pain, I said to my husband that although I had no prior occurrences of this magnitude, I was sure I was in labor. The physician, in a phone consultation, said it sounded like a bladder infection and suggested drinking alcohol. In front of my huge arched window, lying on the floor, still in pain, I drank two to three glasses of Southern Comfort. That "prescription," however, did not quell the pain and I insisted that I be rushed to the hospital. I proceeded to deliver one baby on the floor of the hospital waiting area and the other in the delivery room. My twin girls subsequently died.

For whatever reason, I always demanded it be referred to in the correct medical terms, as an actual live birth. It was neither a miscarriage nor a still birth. Since I was asked to name my daughters and make decisions on burial procedures, at least it seemed that one should acknowledge that the babies were born alive, however brief their lives were.

What I discovered was that the obstetricians responsible for my care were not exactly brimming with appropriate words that might minimally assuage the emotional devastation. As a minor authority in what phrases might offer consolation, it occurred to me that their proficiency was in life, and the death of an infant, or two, created anxiety and a sense of failure. Several years later, I was in the position of helping physicians talk to their patients about many difficult issues in life, which also included death.

Several months after our twins' deaths, I thought I might be pregnant again. It was probably a false bodily deception, a brief abreaction, but I realized that I had not gotten over the prior painful experience. I had not confirmed the pregnancy, so with an undiagnosed serum level, I sought the help of a well-recommended and kind physician in New York. He performed a vacuum aspiration, otherwise known as D and C, to terminate a pregnancy that might or might not have actually been. I had a post check-up with my original physician and mentioned the procedure that occurred. He was verbally reprimanding, critical and punitive because he was fervently against abortion. At that time, my capacity for responses dealing with his hostile attitude was significantly diminished due to my extreme emotional vulnerability and my husband was sent in as a surrogate defender. In retrospect, emotions in moments of crisis, may interfere with reasonable responses. It's "I should have said that." However, he had committed malpractice by ignoring his patient's reports of the possibility of twins. It also is bad medicine not to listen to your patients.

The following year, moody, I vividly remember an event that registered in "black granite," the memory center of the selective brain. Several weeks later, after the death of our twins, my husband invited a friend to visit. He came with one of his numerous girlfriends. She was less than fully functioning, nor fully dressed, and decided to demonstrate her baking acumen. After making brownies, leaving the kitchen a cyclonic mess for an unknown person to clean up, and wearing a sheer, see-through top, close to nudity, they departed. In a car ride later that week, after I complained to my husband about some guests being deleted from our invitation list, or more carefully selected, he commented that I was being oversensitive. In a fury, I jumped out of the car, which was fortunately at a red light, hid in the bushes and walked home at night — a distance of three miles. In that painful loneliness, I deduced that no one, unless they had undergone a very similar experience, could truly empathize with another. And maybe we have been deluded in our belief that spouses, relatives and even well-meaning friends can understand the many lacerations of our individual lives.

There are a multitude of influences that determine the kinds of work our career path will or won't follow. Mammoth journals are written examining this issue and from the point of view of interest, they have been categorized as the most rudimentary shapes. All these factors also influence the outcome of our personal conditions. They are as follows:

Basic Inherited Material (DNA)
- Potential intelligence
- Potential attributes
- Temperament
- Family
- Birth order
- Health

Individual
- Self-worth
- Discipline
- Skills
- Needs (security/acclaim)
- Talent

External
- Spouse
- Luck
- Friends
- Mentors
- Connections
- Income level

With considerable deliberation, I have refrained from re-tracing all the factors that contributed to my personal and professional germination. If I were to tabulate the prior outlined influences and impediments, play roulette with all the combinations, the outcome would be a random speculative excavation into the forces that link one's life experiences.

I was a Behavioral Scientist in a Residency Program for Family Practice residents for ten years. What that nomenclature translated into was that I had the responsibility of teaching family practice residents basic interpersonal skills with patients, explaining the psychological aspects of illness, detecting and understanding emotional problems, as well as the developmental processes in individual and family evolution. The job consisted of far more intensive, diverse and complex functions than found in a written job description. However, to be succinct, during those ten years, one young resident's wife died, a faculty physician and a good friend developed AIDS and died, another resident's baby died of SIDS while she was on call at the hospital, and there was always a guarantee of a caboose of crises.

When the residents or attending physicians evaluated a patient and decided that he or she needed psychological intervention, I was called in to fulfill that responsibility. In my first year at the hospital, another faculty member, in order to make the residents more sensitive to the various aspects of death, interviewed several families of children who had died.

Choosing to examine a proclivity or interest, a rather strange word for the phenomena of death and death's manifestations, there are several conclusions about the determinations of my specialization. Several underlying personal predispositions may be working. It is extremely gratifying to ease one's suffering. Even as aptly labeled, the last dance to which we all will be invited, the intimacy, the emotional movement, and the growth that occurs with the dying or to the people who remain allows me not to avoid this truth or suffering, and to participate in the sequence of one's transformation, both the dying and mine.

Being closely attached to the world of physicians, I naturally acquired the experience of frequent exposure to death. A family physician had referred to me an attractive young female patient (19 years old), from a warm, close family. As is characteristic of teenagers, she was troubled because an unresolved relationship with a boy had caused some depression and anxiety. The short-term treatment goal was to help her accept that her boyfriend wanted to date other females. Several months later, her physician told her that she had cancer, theoretically the most successfully treatable variety. When visiting her at Sloan-Kettering one and one-half years later, the most unfathomable, inevitable realization shocked me. I felt like the Munch painting, "The Scream." I had denied the truth. She died weeks later. And that was my first orientation in the so-called sub-specialty of Children Dying.

Subsequently, deaths of all ages entered my life and office. I have seen patients whose cancer has taken on a perverse form. One of the more physically grotesque was a man whose tumor grew out of his head, a replica of the "elephant man," distorting his face into ugliness that affected his speech.

And thus I became the precursor to obituary writing, the archeologist of passages towards death: AIDS, cancer, suicide, car accidents, death by a supermarket truck, and all the illnesses of youth. So many did not die of old age.

This direct education in dying and grief has sometimes put things into a unique perspective that enables me to respond to certain events with more equanimity. Yet, at times, I admit that I sink into the usual daily complaints and angry reactions when I believe that I've been unjustly treated. I do try to reflect on how remarkable it is that, with humor and composure, so many of my friends and patients have faced their deaths.

Due to family needs, a growing private practice, and an urge to modify habitual working, a tendency to be a workaholic, I chose a simplification course and I left the residency program.

For three years, my private practice was very gratifying. However, when my husband retired, this hiatus was discontinued. At the time of writing this book, I have the title of Director of Behavioral Science at another residency program. The challenge is a two hour commute each way on the train. That time accounts for my attempts at writing, volumes of reading and a protected period of reflection to decide what constitutes "doing the right thing."

CHAPTER 13

Epilogue

I've written short pieces on weighty subjects that require acres of continuing analysis. The importance of these issues varies tremendously from person to person, depending upon what has occurred in the sequences of their lives.

At the core of these essays is the supposition that implicit attitudes and persistent thoughtful behavior should be revived. Inherent in these sentiments is that most of us can be more discerning and skillful in some aspects of our lives. The pertinent questions have always been the same. One might envision that our own personal vaccine for improvement may be listening better, choosing to participate in an ethical decision, being generous, or not taking advantage of others. The diseases of our times range from freedom without values, to selfishness, floods of indulgences, and obsessive self-centeredness.

There is no particular reason that I have omitted major headliners such as sex (although it sells), AIDS, spirituality, and the continual shifts in media popularity. I attribute the deletion of sex to the fact that is has reached a saturation point in the perpetual disclosures, voluntary and involuntary spying that occurs both in front of and behind the scenes. The inane confessional displays of sexual checkerboards should be straightjacketed away before these secretions cause intense allergic re-actions.

I realize that other areas are as urgent as the ones I have concentrated on, and their exclusion is not intended to lessen the extreme importance of considering them. This was just an idiosyncratic determinant on my part.

Embedded in these chapters, however, is a sincere concern about salvaging relationships with others and with oneself. In today's turbulent and unsettled times, both are in a dispersing mess. The demands we face are not easy to handle and the choices we make and inclinations require serious commitments.

It is up to the reader to ferret out some meaning in these ideas and determine the particular application that will be most beneficial in his or her commerce of living. A counterpart to the better judgments we need to discern is the drainage caused by the misuse of alcohol in our society and on our youth, and its capricious impairment for couples and families.

Like a thorny weed, or demented rumblings, my concern with habitual alcohol consumption appears again. It is seductive, particularly for women who are vulnerable. The drinking landscape is more opaque, unseen by others. Drinking soothes loneliness or depression. It is an attempt to obliterate something — painful events or memories — and has the ability to quell rage and allows the drinker to hover away from the world.

It has a benign beginning and a tragic end. Alcohol is impervious to logic. The consistent use of alcohol is the initiation of a huge loan, edging one closer and closer to the proximity of bankruptcy in both personal and professional areas.

Although I have discussed this in a prior chapter, it is worthy, at least in my estimation, of another go-round. If you think about the "A" word frequently, or drink alcohol on a regular basis, or binge, thinking all the while that life is not fun without it, there may be a problem stalking you. When yearning and craving are present, it is another sign that the deception is upon you.

There are several ways you can determine if alcohol is becoming a problem. Refrain from drinking for a month. Develop strategies that help promote an alcohol-free month. Make an honest statement to yourself and others that *you are not drinking* for a month. *It is the truth.* A while ago, I mentioned this abstinence activity to a woman I had just met, and her reply was "I could never do that." Flag's at half mast! This was a real clue to her addiction to alcohol. She was also the daughter of an alcoholic. I am uncomfortable, however, confronting anyone about their indulgences, especially with people I do not know well.

There is a caveat to this abstinence plan. If you are a heavy drinker, which I characterize as more than three glasses per day, a medical consultation should be considered prior to abstinence because of possible withdrawal symptoms.

In states of inebriation, characterized by the absence of truly conscious thoughts, one is not charmings nor a delight. More spectacles of pathetic behavior are likely to occur. It gives everyone around a person in this condition the uneasy feeling that a disaster is impending, an accurate forewarning.

It is also very difficult to predict who will pass through the fine line — that invisible prime meridian — and arrive at alcoholism. One's interior monologue always deceives one by saying such devious things as: "You can always stop;" "Other people drink as much as you;" "It's the social thing to do." Eventually, the truth gets drowned out and it's all reduced to: "I need it, I deserve it, something will kill me anyway." The fact is that one who believes that he or she cannot live without alcohol, that it's necessary for calming crises, for soothing the soul, for relaxation and a treatment for every emotional challenge is a person who is "hooked."

The problems that people have presented to me in my practice as a therapist can be placed on a scale from those of epic disease proportions to the minor malarias of dissatisfactions with others and themselves. The solutions are not thermodynamic. I have offered some common antidotes to the themes that punctuate each chapter.

They are my prejudices. Implement only one of the ideas suggested in the chapters or at least take some time to reflect on your giving quotients, your abilities to listen and if you do nothing directly or inadvertently, you can retain any old behavior or cancel your moral subscription. Bad actions are always renewable.

There is nothing revolutionary in these suggestions. It is generally a healthy psychological supplement to be immersed in a project: baking a cake, sewing curtains, making a personal card, building a deck. Passive watching subtracts from substantial accomplishments. Our alliance with machinery impedes our development within ourselves and concomitantly with others.

I advocate times of muteness. When you are with others, relinquish the impenetrable self-focused barriers by decreasing your speed of interrupting and concentrate on someone else. Can the concerns of others teach you anything? Are you able to unscramble their codes, fears and the life cavities that perturb them? By probing others and foregoing your own dilemmas, you may replenish yourself favorably.

With this concept in mind, practice classifying yourself in the silent submarine service and the periscope may lead to solutions previously obscure. When you are alone, remove all impediments that will interfere with beginning or completing a project. Delete all possibilities for television, and other routes to entering the dominion of inert thinking — the fax, phones, and computer. Fortify yourself while under the siege of interruptions.

Attachments that anchor and provide comfort are the people and places that guide our search. The loyalty of friends, the love and continuity with our children are the work that is most important. The way we conduct ourselves in all the daily expressions are our lasting performances.

__When you are dead, what do you want__
__people to say about you?__

Concluding Advice

1. Do not assume that you get credit for past behavior. The brain registers what one *doesn't* do.
2. Assuming that others in our personal and professional lives act in accordance with our values generally leads to disappointment. Some do, some don't.
3. The most dramatic conflicts are perhaps those occurring in the solitary mind.
4. Only in adversity can one really know whom to trust.
5. Anger need not always be expressed.
6. Failure is not trying.
7. Negative comments register stronger than positive.
8. Happiness, as an end, is as elusive as handling mercury from a broken thermometer.
9. The unexamined life is not worth living, yet the overexamined life is *not* living.
10. We do not always re-create the pathology of our family; we sometimes design our own.
11. Deeds are more important than words. There are no rewards for what you intend to do.
12. Generosity is as beneficial to the giver as to the receiver.
13. An enduring gift is the recommendation of a good book.
14. People can do something to you in one instant that changes something forever.
15. The ability to understand someone profoundly outweighs giving advice.

16. Send your narcissism to the cleaners and do not pick it up for a month.

17. Failures of communication are a result of dismal listening.

18. Practice times of muteness; learning might take place.

19. Do not expect from marriage what it can't rebate.

20. Tell your friends what you like about them.

Appreciation

I wish to thank my daughter, son and husband who have tolerated my disappearing acts in and out of the house. They have respected my need for solitude and time alone.

Several of my friends read the initial drafts in the early stages of the book and made some valuable suggestions. Others have always given their support in numerous ways. They have encouraged me to "be as I am." In alphabetical order they are:

Dr. Susan Bauman, Family Physician
Frankie Cadwell, President of Advertising Agency
Beverlee Ciccone, PhD., Psychologist
Rhoda Feingenbaum, PhD, Psychologist
Susan Fineman, Teacher and Writer
Susie Hilfiger, Clothing Designer
Harriet Plavoukos, Business Woman, Real Estate

The services of a commissioned editor, Shirley Longshore, have been greatly appreciated. Stephanie Schneider, the Director of Medical Informatics at the Crozer Family Practice Residency Programs, has been an invaluable asset in editing, revisions and sharing my particular humor.

Of course, there are additional thanks to family, my sister especially, unmentioned friends, patients, professional associates and others that have offered their stories. If I have inadvertently omitted anyone, they will appear in my next book.

About the Author

    For over 30 years Dr. Chiesa has been an educator, psychologist, workshop presenter, mother and wife. She is a lively communicator whose sense of humor encourages ethical relationships and ways to think about our major life decisions. Dr. Chiesa is available for conferences, speaking engagements, workshops, lunch time discussions for corporations, universities, and charitable organizations. Your comments and questions are welcome.

She can be reached at: (215) 862-2653
1 (800) 434-9888
Email Address: mchiesa@crozer.org

Or you can contact the   **Independent Psychology Press**
P.O. Box 12
Stockton, NJ 08559